Breakthrough Into Renewal
How a traditional church caught a sense of mission...

David Haney

BROADMAN PRESS
NASHVILLE, TENNESSEE

DEDICATION
In Memory Of
DAVID G. BALES
who gave me
my mother
LUCILLE BALES
HANEY
and a family of
aunts and uncles
LENORA BALES
EARL BALES
JOHN BALES
DONALD BALES

© Copyright 1974 • Broadman Press
All rights reserved
4255-45
ISBN: 0-8054-5545-0

Library of Congress Catalog Card Number: 73-93905
Dewey Decimal Classification:
Printed in the United States of America

FOREWORD

Fresh winds are blowing amongst the churches today. Hunger for deeper spiritual experiences and a longing for the joy of exciting fellowship have cnouraged many believers and church members to seek the path of serious renewal. The new winds, blowing across arid areas, determine to place a new spring in the step of the believer, a new song on the lips of the discouraged and a new satisfying relationship in the empty heart. For an age of insecurity, of moral questioning, and—in too many cases—of hopeless spiritual defeat, here comes a breakthrough in answer: fulfilling spiritual joy and victory is granted by God as his people seek and work in the effort to know him fully.

Breakthrough is a scintillating journey by a pastor and a people into real and vital discovery. It is the discovery there is more in the Christian's personal relationship to the Holy Spirit. Further, the pages tell that discovery came to bear in experience wraught by pain, disillusionment and often those well-intentioned criticisms. Yet experience bore toward the joyfully reality of a church renewed and fulfilling the role of a ministry equipped to do that which is assigned by the Lord.

Dear Reader, you may not agree with all which comes from the experiences of this church, but you must note the serious journey embarked on by the pastor and people. That which is written here is neither an absolute example nor criteria of renewal: it does say to us, however, that through the struggles, renewal can take place with joy and satisfaction. These winds are blowing all over. How good to see our Lord continuing to work in creative ministry—and in Heritage Baptist Church!

C. B. Hogue, *Director*
Division of Evangelism
Home Mission Board, SBC

CONTENTS

PROLOGUE	ix
1. IN FRONT OF THE SUN, THE CLOUDS ARE ALWAYS BLOCKING	11
2. ON YOUR MARK, GET SET, GO! BUT WHERE?	21
3. A LONG DAY'S JOURNEY INTO LIGHT	35
4. MEANWHILE, BACK AT THE RANCH	47
5. ONE STEP FORWARD, TWO STEPS BACK	63
6. COME ON IN, THE WATER'S FINE	76
7. AND THEY CAME BEARING GIFTS	84
8. DEEP AND WIDE, DEEP AND WIDE	92
9. EVERY MOUNTAIN HAS FOUR VALLEYS	101
10. WHERE NEXT, FOR CHRIST'S SAKE?	110
EPILOGUE	117
APPENDIXES	124

READING LIST

Anderson, Philip. *Church Meetings That Matter.* Philadelphia: United Church Press. 1965.
Barclay, William, ed. *The Revelation of John.* Philadelphia: Westminster Press, 1961.
Casteel, John. *Spiritual Renewal Through Personal Groups.* New York: Association Press, 1967.
Clemmons, William and Hester, Harvey. *Growth Through Groups.* Nashville: Broadman Press, 1974.
Drakeford, John. *Farewell to the Lonely Crowd.* Waco: Word, Inc., 1969.
Edge, Findley. *The Greening of the Church.* Waco: Word, Inc., 1972.
Erdman, Charles. *The Revelation of John.* Philadelphia: Westminster Press, 1936.
Girard, Robert. *Brethren, Hang Loose.* Grand Rapids: Zondervan, 1973.
Haney, David. *The Idea of the Laity.* Grand Rapids: Zondervan, 1973.
_____. *Renew My Church.* Grand Rapids: Zondervan, 1972.
Kelly, Thomas. *A Testament of Devotion.* New York: Harper and Row, 1941.
Larson, Bruce. *Dare to Live Now.* Grand Rapids: Zondervan, 1967.
_____. *Living on the Growing Edge.* Grand Rapids: Zondervan, 1968.
_____. *No Longer Strangers.* Waco: Word, Inc., 1971.
_____. *Setting Men Free.* Grand Rapids: Zondervan, 1967.
Larson, Bruce and Osborne, Ralph. *The Emerging Church.* Waco: Word, Inc., 1970.
Mahoney, James. *Journey into Fullness.* Nashville: Broadman Press, 1974.
Miller, Keith. *A Second Touch.* Waco: Word, Inc., 1967.
_____. *The Taste of New Wine.* Waco: Word, Inc., 1965.
Miller, Paul. *Group Dynamics in Evangelism.* Scottsdale: Herald Press, 1958.
Morris, Colin. *Include Me Out.* Nashville: Abingdon Press, 1968.
Mullen, Thomas. *The Renewal of the Ministry.* Nashville: Abingdon Press, 1963.
Neighbour, Ralph W., Jr. *The Seven Last Words of the Church.* Grand Rapids: Zondervan, 1973.
_____. *The Touch of the Spirit.* Nashville: Broadman Press, 1973.
O'Connor, Elizabeth. *Call to Commitment.* New York: Harper and Row, 1963.
_____. *The Eighth Day of Creation.* Waco: Word, 1971.
Paxon, Ruth. *Life on the Highest Plane.* Chicago: Moody Press, 1928.
Reid, Clyde. *Groups Alive—Church Alive.* New York: Harper and Row, 1969.
Rinker, Rosalind. *Prayer: Conversing with God.* Grand Rapids, Zondervan.
Shoemaker, Samuel. *Extraordinary Living for Ordinary Men.* Grand Rapids: Zondervan, 1965.
Smith, Hannah Whitehall. *The Christian's Secret of a Happy Life.* Westwood, N.J.: Revell, 1970.
Steere, Douglas. *On Beginning from Within.* New York: Harper and Row, 1964.
Taylor, Jack. *The Key to Triumphant Living.* Nashville: Broadman, 1971.
Trueblood, Elton. *A Place to Stand.* New York: Harper and Row, 1969.
_____. *The Company of the Committed.* New York: Harper and Row, 1961.
_____. *Foundations for Reconstruction.* Waco: Word, Inc., 1973. New York: Harper and Row, 1946; revised 1961.
_____. *The Incendiary Fellowship.* New York: Harper and Row, 1967.
_____. *The New Man for Our Time.* New York: Harper and Row, 1970.
Bender, Urie. *The Witness.* Scottsdale: Herald Press, 1965.

PROLOGUE
(Please Read!)

Breakthrough into Renewal is a first-person report of a renewal experiment in an existing congregation: the Heritage Baptist Church of Annapolis, Maryland. Because of this, there are several important implications to the reader.

First, Heritage is an *existing* congregation, with roots extending back to pre-Civil War days. Thus, the report is valuable in that most of the renewal writing about actual church situations to date has been about *new* congregations initiated with renewal concepts as the foundation. While these efforts and the consequent reports have been immeasurably beneficial, they have not had to hurdle the barricades of longstanding *tradition*. This represents the interim report of a congregation who started with the accumulated weight of more than a century.

Second, it is the report of *our* church. Thus, there is a notable absence of documentation and footnotes from other sources and renewal reports. This was a deliberate choice in that no attempt is made to either defend or support our efforts by appealing to what others have done or said. In truth, we are debtors to nearly every renewal report in print, but this constitutes *our contribution*.

Third, it is a *first person* report and, hence, the first person singular is used far more than I (there it is) could wish. My (again!) first two books, *Renew My Church* and *The Idea of the Laity*, are more my (yet, again) "style." Yet, my (another) own pilgrimage is so intertwined with that of the Heritage Church, it made any other choice impossible.

Fourth, it is the report of a *Baptist* church. In previous writings, it has been my attempt to speak to the wider audience of evangelicals, hence, a wider vocabulary. This book, however, speaks "Baptist" and this may be a bit different to the other-than-Baptist reader.

Finally, a word about *style*. The purpose of *Breakthrough into Renewal* is two-fold. First, it is the simple sharing of the chronological story. But, there is another purpose—that of sharing not only where we've been, but *what we've learned*. Thus, there are sections in nearly every chapter which begin, "Parenthetically speaking. . . ." These represent truths, suggestions, and explanations which we can faithfully pass along to others.

At this writing, we are beginning our seventh year together as a pastor and a people. We pray, however, that it will not be a sabbath year of rest. Rather, our prayer is that it be a year of Jubilee in which the captives of tradition are everywhere set free.

1. IN FRONT OF THE SUN, THE CLOUDS ARE ALWAYS BLOCKING

But Elijah went a day's journey into the wilderness, and came and sat down under a broom tree; and he asked that he might die, saying, "It is enough; now, O Lord, take away my life; for I am no better than my fathers" (1 Kings 19:4).

Disillusionment is more like a fog than a storm, and I suppose that explains why I do not know when it really started. The disillusionment with my life and ministry, I mean. I do know when it began to be *apparent*, however; it was shortly after I had come to a small, newly established Baptist church in 1962 at New Lebanon, Ohio, a suburb of Dayton.

My conversion came at the age of sixteen when, as best as I knew how, I asked Christ to come into my life and to straighten the tangles a typical teenager usually makes on his own. Almost simultaneously came my "call to preach," a deep sense of direction that this was to be the path for me.

My first sermon was preached in my father's pulpit at the Urbancrest Baptist Church in Lebanon, Ohio, on my mother's birthday, August 21, 1955.[1] The next month, I enrolled at Harrison-Chilhowee Baptist Academy near Knoxville, Tennessee, graduating in 1957. During that time I was given a "boy-wonder" image—a sixteen-year-old preacher enjoying considerable success as a youth evangelist, preaching every Saturday night in a "skid-row" mission and in sixteen church crusades.

Aileen and I were married shortly after graduation and I enrolled at Georgetown College in Kentucky, graduating as a religion major in 1961. During my four years there I served as a student pastor at the Sadieville Baptist Church, just north of Georgetown—again enjoying good success and preaching widely in revivals and rallies.

Following graduation, I enrolled at Southeastern Baptist Theological Seminary in Wake Forest, North Carolina, but withdrew after one semester to accept the call to the New Lebanon Church, with the intention of transfering to the Southern Baptist Theological Seminary in Louisville, Kentucky.

By that time, our family had grown to include Karen, born in 1959, and Steven, born in 1960. We moved to New Lebanon with considerable anticipation and delight. Not only was the church a "good opportunity"—a new church in an exploding community—but we were moving back "home": both of our families lived in the Dayton area.

What happened next only reinforced the ascribed "boy-wonder" image. That first Sunday saw eighty or so in Sunday School and an offering of about $125. In a matter of months, it was nearly two hundred in Sunday School with $500 offerings! And, it continued in just that fashion, month after month. It was a surprise to no one that shortly thereafter I was elected moderator of the then seventy-one-church Greater Dayton Association of Baptists—at the ripe old age of twenty-six. A year later, at the age of twenty-seven, I was elected president of the Ohio Baptist Pastor's Conference.

By this time I had preached in some fifty-three church crusades in thirteen states in ten years. It was about then that the fog began to gather. I sensed it, but refused to admit it.

The possibility of commuting to the seminary in Louisville and staying on campus four days each week had now been precluded. Both the growth of the church and my denominational involvement would not permit it. I then began to search for other graduate schools or seminary possibilites. One of them was Earlham College, a Quaker school just across the state line in nearby Richmond, Indiana. Their response was a "turning point." They had just started a new seminary on campus and *Elton Trueblood* would be teaching in it as well as at the college where he had taught for a quarter of a century. And only forty-five minutes away! I enrolled in September of 1963, commuting every other day, until my residency was completed in 1967.

But, the fog only thickened. And, more importantly, I began to admit it. A major factor in it was the Earlham emphasis on the pastor being the "equipper" of the saints—a striking contrast to one conditioned to view the pastor as the entertaining-enterprising-evangelist! (*Entertaining*—"keep 'em happy"; *enterprising*—"keep 'em going"; *evangelist*—"keep 'em coming.")

When the fog fully arrived, it came all at once. I began to admit some things and to become aware of some others. It was 1965, the only bright spot of which was the birth of our third child, Philip. And I was sick. Sick of myself. I began to see and to admit my own spiritual shallowness. My praying was irregular and impersonal; my Bible reading was either class preparation or sermon hunting; my attitude was judgmental and superior to a fault. And, yet, by every other standard, I was a "success" in the ministry! That in itself told me something was wrong, *bad* wrong, with either me or the ministry. It was both.

Added to this was a growing disillusionment with "gimmicks": like playing on emotions to get public decisions—if not for conversion, then for "rededication"—or to "pray daily," to be a "better father," or *whatever* got them down the aisle. "Numbers" was the name of the game, the symbols of success.

I began to study the Gospels in desperation during this time, and I could not help but notice the contrast of Christ's style with mine—his open, honest, loving, accepting calls to *discipleship* over against my subtle trickery to get *decisions*. Yet the necessity to produce statistics to support the image of success literally imprisoned me.

Likewise, I was growing sick of the church; not just mine, but Christianity in general. Knowing my own authenticity was wanting, I looked to other Christians for some hint of it. I saw very little to encourage. In fact, I only saw myself, magnified and multiplied many times over: the same shallowness existed in "key" laymen as it did among "key" preachers. (Salt was poured in my wound when, at a conference during this time, I heard a speaker say,

"Most churches are merely the spiritual extensions of their pastors.") All around me was the same statistics-success-syndrome. But, I was learning that "statistics" can never satisfy the spirit of man; man is not a computer. Holding office, building buildings, raising budgets, adding members, does not—will not—*cannot* satisfy! Indeed, it only breeds a bigger appetite for the same things and, paradoxically, produces *dissatisfaction.*

My pastoral "problems" were not the sin in the community nor broken, hurting lives in need of healing. Rather, they were criticism over omitting a couple of names on the list of Vacation Bible School workers; editorials in a neighboring pastor's newsletter about my "stealing his sheep"; a clique forming around a Sunday School teacher who complained about being replaced by the nominating committee which he "couldn't believe" even though he had missed twenty-six of fifty-two Sundays the previous year; and a thousand other similar "crises." (An additional problem during times like these is to identify the whole of a congregation with the few negative examples!) And, the overwhelming thrust of it was the *pettiness* of it all—while the world went to hell. Was this *Christianity?*

By 1967, the fog which became visible in 1965, had become thick enough to obscure everything else. The disillusionment Aileen and I both now felt, was deepened by the death of my father. After thirty years of serving churches and erecting buildings, he simply "wore out" at only fifty-nine. *And for what?* That's exactly what I asked.

And, I was tired, *physically* tired. Going to school, two building programs in five years, preaching three times a week, conducting four outside meetings every spring and fall, coupled with the spiritual and professional disillusionment was too much. It was then that I came to a mutually-exclusive conclusion: (1) There had to be more to Christianity than I had or could see or (2) I was going to get out of the ministry!

My decision, however, was to give it another try. Frankly, I was too embarrassed and/or afraid to quit! I had graduated "with honors" from the Earlham School of Religion; all of my training had been in religion and I was not prepared for another vocation. And, besides, *what would people think?* The people in the church, my pastor friends, my classmates; I had neither the energy nor the gall to face them.

The pastorate was not all, I knew, so I began to pursue the (for me) "cop out" route of "other ministries"—teaching religion, student work, denominational work, *anything*. But, nothing opened. Nothing! It was *unbelievable!* Here I was, the "boy-wonder," a "success" at twenty-six, graduated with honors under *Elton Trueblood?* no less—and I couldn't even get a nibble! I solicited my friends, sent applications, prayed, called, wrote—and *nothing!*

Then, an idea began to emerge: maybe, just maybe, it was *God* doing the blocking! There was no other obvious explanation for it. I sensed that God had something to say to me. I dreaded it, but I knew the time had come.

Meanwhile, there was a church in Maryland also undergoing the process of divine-disillusionment: the College Avenue Baptist Church (now the Heritage Baptist Church) in Annapolis.[2]

It was a church with a momentous past—which was at least a part of their problem: living on momentum of the past. As the "downtown" Baptist Church in Maryland's capital, it dated back to 1857 when the first short-lived attempt was made to initiate the church. The Civil War interrupted its story and in the 1880's a second short-lived attempt was made. It was not until 1899 that a lasting work developed. From then on it was a miracle story of growth, building, and influence.

During its first fifty or so years, Heritage sent out a foreign missionary, a number of ministerial students, built a beautiful stone building across the street from the capital building, and started five new churches. Through its contributions and leadership involvement, Heritage also grew in denominational stature, becoming one of the key churches in the Baptist Convention of Maryland. Particularly significant was the fact that Heritage sponsored the Manhattan Baptist Church in New York City out of which grew the Baptist Convention (Southern) of New York.

Like many other churches, Heritage enjoyed the "boom" years of the fifties when churches everywhere were exploding in attendance. But, other explosions began occuring, too, and the clouds of disillusionment began to gather. Sorting back through it all is still painful, but enough is evident to expose an all too familiar pattern.

First, the city of Annapolis began to change. Until 1950 or so, Annapolis was a cultured, provincial community of twenty-five thousand, highly prizing its rich history as a pre-Revolutionary War city. Most of the downtown buildings and houses still date back to the early 1700's. It was here that the colonial Congress gathered many times, where Lafayette was entertained, where Washington resigned his commission as Commander of the Revolutionary Army, and where the Treaty of Paris was ratified, officially ending the Revolution. But, change came. The cities of Washington and Baltimore began to overflow and Annapolis became a bedroom city for both. New insurance offices opened, a cluster of research laboratories gathered, new businesses came; and each brought more new people to Annapolis.

One problem could well be labeled: "from provincial to cosmopolitan." This, in turn, brought new people into the churches. And, slowly across the 1950's and early 1960's, it had its effect on the life-style of Heritage. Definite groups, bordering on cliques, began to emerge: the original church families and the new families, the latter subdivided into a "new-but-loyal" Southern Baptist group and a "new-but-independent" group, many from other denominational backgrounds. The sad element is that, as best as all can now assess, they were all good, well-intentioned, loyal members; just unaware of exactly what it was that was "different" about the others.

Then, there was a problem of debt. During the boom years of the mid-1950's, Heritage's sudden growth indicated needed educational space, and a three-story unit was added. As was true all across the nation, however, the growth did not continue; in fact, like many others, it subsided. The debt was assumed with anticipated financial growth which did not come. Financial concerns then became both an added problem and a cause of friction, plus the disillusionment of not seeing the anticipated growth. At times, blame was placed internally, rather than on societal change.

This did not make for the best pastoral conditions and, from

1953 to 1966, there were four pastorates averaging three years each. The church's ministry to the Baptist midshipmen at the United States Naval Academy dated back to 1904, but the 1950's also brought growth in it, too. A full-time student ministry was added, but succession was the story there, also. An unworkable joint effort of the denomination and the church created supervising problems and leadership conflicts, again leading to disillusionment with a well-intentioned desire to minister.

By 1967, this decade and a half of disillusionment had taken its toll. Several key families left the church. Other families stayed, but dropped either or both their financial and spiritual support. After several heated business meetings, attempts to gain blocks of power, and breeches of fellowship within the newly appointed pulpit committee, the clouds hung low. The people knew there had to be more than this to Christianity. But where and how?

It was then that, one by one, members and families began to pray *in earnest*—without any concerted effort or organized encouragement—about their own spiritual lives, the life of the church, and mostly, for a pastor.

The year, 1967, found me in much the same position and posture, too. There had to be more. But where and how? V. Raymond Edman says it is a familiar pattern for individuals. We also know now it is true for churches as well.

They had believed on the Savior, yet they were burdened and bewildered, unfaithful and unfruitful, always yearning for a better way and never achieving by their efforts a better life. Then they came to a crisis of utter heart surrender to the Savior, a meeting with Him in the innermost depths of their spirit; and they found the Holy Spirit to be an unfailing fountain of life and refreshment. Thereafter life was never again the same. . . . New life had been exchanged for old.

The pattern seems to be: self-centeredness, self-effort, increasing inner dissatisfaction and outer discouragement, a temptation to give it all up because there is no better way; and then finding the Spirit of God to be their strength, their guide, their confidence and companion—in a word, their life.[3]

The disillusionment-become-disgust with my own spiritual life and the institutional church, along with superficial Christians, denominational politics, and, above all, the pastorate, reached a climax about the beginning of 1967 and, perhaps, centered around the death of my father. Dead at fifty-nine. Worn-out. Unheralded. *What was it worth?* There *had* to be worth to such a life. But, how?

It was then that the sun began to break through *my* clouds, not enough to light the whole terrain, but at least enough to illuminate some landmarks. One was spiritual, one personal, and another, vocational. Looking back on them, I frankly cannot remember their chronological sequence; it is likely that they can only be separated theoretically.

One night I had gathered with a group of fellow pastors and guest preachers. A citywide evangelistic effort was underway in all the area churches, and we had gathered together to pray for it. It was my first introduction to "conversational prayer" (to be discussed later) and the first time (I think) that I ever "broke through" into a *personal* relationship with Christ.

Don't misunderstand me: I had been "converted"; I had accepted him as my "personal Savior"; but, I had never entered into a meaningful *personal* relationship with him. He was always "out there" and "other than" to me. As with any personal encounter, it is difficult to describe or analyze, but, somehow, I knew I had met him that night and had seen a side of him I had not known before. He cared for *me.* He knew what I was going through; *all along*, he knew it! *But, he couldn't start until I quit!* To this day, only one of the dozen men present knew what was going on in my life: they were praying about Christ's crusade in the city; I was praying about Christ's crusade in me!

What happened? In short, I named him "Lord" of my life, my destiny, my ministry. He did not force me to do it, however; he did not have to. I suddenly realized that he cared more about all of it than I did myself! And, what is more, he was able to do something about it. I was now willing to trust him, not only with my soul, but my *life*, too. I realized that he knew, better than I, what I was to do and how I was to do it.

Then, another previously unmanagable piece also fell into place: I not only discovered him, I discovered "me." My ministry to date—preaching, visiting, administering, and so forth—had always been a composite of imitations. Unwilling to trust myself, I watched others who were "successful" and imitated them! In this process of discovery, I somehow came to see that God loved *me;* that God had created *me;* that God had called *me;* and I started trying to be *me* for a change. Not the as-is *me,* but the one he created me *to be.*

I was not the "David Haney" God had *created;* I was the one I had *compiled.* I do not know that one can ever "arrive" in this process of becoming, but it makes life and living a dynamically creative adventure, and I am increasingly convinced that the salvation-life is essentially a call *to become.* It is a summons to begin the redemptive process of being made "complete" and "whole," as the Bible words it. This allowed me to view my strengths and weaknesses, my besetting sins and my personal set of temptations and to begin to let him deal with them appropriately. Having made the start, I began to see the "me" in me and, quite candidly, I began to enjoy being God's "me."

Finally, my view of the pastorate changed. No words are really adequate to express my total disillusionment with it as holding any hope for the God Movement. But, as actively as I pursued other options, every door closed as soon as I turned up the walk! Being willing to trust him and beginning to find "me," allowed the recognition on my part that God wanted *me* in the *pastorate.* Funny, but I accepted it with no difficulty at all!

But, "staying in the pastorate" was not the same in my mind as "staying in the pastorate" *where I was!* "Any place but here," I said! I prayed and prayed for another church. Nothing opened. *Nothing!* (I still had not learned that prayer is not trying to talk God into something or to persuade him against his will; rather, it is giving him a chance to talk us into some things and an opportunity to persuade us!)

A friend was visiting in our church at the time, leading a teacher-training emphasis for us. Before the session one evening, we prayed together. With evident discernment, he prayed, "God, help Dave to be satisfied where he is." I did not hear another thing he said all evening. Just that phrase: "where he is." And my heart kept responding, "That's it!" That was the key.

The lordship of Christ means he is in control, and peace is the result of our obedience, where we are, wherever we are! And, with an ease which defies explanation, I accepted my role, *where I was*, with a determination to be used *then* and *there*. That was Wednesday. Thursday and Friday saw me as a new pastor. I actually enjoyed being where and what I was for the first time in two years. The future suddenly looked unbelievably enticing. I was literally and miraculously *excited* about staying!

That weekend, *five* pulpit committees contacted me!

One of them was from the Heritage Baptist Church of Annapolis, Maryland.

Notes

All Scripture quotations are from the Revised Standard Version unless otherwise indicated.

1. My father, the Rev. George G. Haney, entered the ministry late in life, serving as mission-pastor, starting new churches. In the thirty years of his ministry, he started new Baptist churches in Lebanon and South Lebanon, Ohio, and served as pastor in Miamisburg, Ohio. He died in 1967 at the age of fifty-nine.

2. As this book will reveal, the College Avenue name was changed in 1972 when we relocated to the "Heritage Baptist Church." From 1899 to 1903, it was named "The Baptist Church of Annapolis." Throughout the balance of the book, "Heritage" is used for the sake of uniformity.

3. Edman V. Raymond, *They Found the Secret* (Grand Rapids): Zondervan, 1960), "Introduction."

2. ON YOUR MARK, GET SET, GO! BUT WHERE?

By faith Abraham obeyed when he was called to go out to a place which he was to receive as an inheritance; and he went out, not knowing where he was to go (Heb. 11:8).

While the initial contact from Heritage Church came in the late spring of 1967, personal commitments, vacations, and several meetings with the pulpit committee delayed my official coming until October. Somehow, during our consultations, we were both able to be honest about our *mutual disillusionments*. Also, my statement of *personal objectives* in the ministry met with such obvious approval that it was difficult to miss the "match" God had plotted for us. At best, these *personal objectives* were "uncataloged ideas." They were individually clear, but they were as yet independent of each other. The meshing of the ideas was to come through experience.

The basic idea was that before Christ's church could go further, it had to go deeper. Both of us recognized that.

The second directional idea had to do with *evangelism*. A church, as a Christian, is called to witness. We have our *raison d'etre* only as we discover that function. "Follow me," Jesus said, "and I will make you fishers of men"; and we cannot separate the *call* from the *commission*. He calls us for a distinct *purpose!* Their disillusionment with "high-pressure" evangelism, however, matched mine. There had to be a more wholesome, Christ-like approach to it, one which coupled commitment to conversion and discipleship to decision. The "fruit" Christ wants to produce through us is to be the kind which "remains."

They, too, had seen too many come-and-go "converts" and here-and-gone "revivals." So many potential converts had been "turned off" by previous high-pressure revivals at Heritage Church that the members were refusing to bring their friends anymore. (We did not, however, give up on revivals immediately. We tried two per year for three years, reaching a total of *seven* new members! Then, we faced up to it: revivalism, as a major *outreach* tool, was ineffective *here*. From all reports, however, "revivalism" is not an ineffective tool for evangelism everywhere. In some places, it is; in others, it is very effective.) How our assigned task of evangelism was best to be done was not known to either the church or me, but we both knew that both the *depth* and the *style* of our evangelism had to change.

Another of those uncataloged ideas had to do with the *basic premise* of the renewal movement: that the church will be renewed in our time only as the laity become ministers. Our best hope lies in the *abolition* of the laity, when *all* believers are seen as ministers.

A corollary of the "lay ministry" idea is the "equipping ministry" of the pastor. That is, biblically, there is only one category of Christians: *ministers*. Within that category, however, are various functions, one of which is the *pastoral* ministry. The function of the pastoral minister is that of "equipping the ministers" to carry out their own callings.[1] Five pastors (including me) and two student ministers in twelve years, regardless of the explanations, made Heritage at least "open" to a new view of the pastoral ministry!

Finally, there was one personal idea; an idea about the renewal of the church which had emerged in my own set of orienting maxims: that renewal must take place in *existing* churches, not new, experimental ones. These experimental churches were obviously necessary in that existing churches were failing to cut new paths. These experiments in renewal, then, became our "models"; models indicating what could be done and how. But, the answer to renewal does not lie in the proliferation of new, experimental churches. This ignores the *existing* churches in need of renewal! Merely to initiate new churches is not renewal: it is simply new.

With these ideas to guide us, we began our journey on Sunday October 15, 1967. It was formalized on November 12, 1967, with an installation service led by Dr. Carl F. H. Henry, then editor of *Christianity Today*, on whom I had written my thesis while at the Earlham School of Religion.

Three months later, in January, 1968, we took the first step in the renewal journey. Prior to my coming to Heritage Church in October, I had asked Dr. James Mahoney to come for a "Deeper Life Conference." He agreed and the dates were set: January 14-20, 1968. I prefaced his coming with two messages on the Spirit-filled life to familiarize the people with the concept and the vocabulary. Dr. Mahoney started on Sunday morning. By Friday night, a church had literally been turned around.

DEFINITIONS

PARENTHETICALLY SPEAKING, "renewal" and "the deeper life" are not synonymous. *Renewal* is an "idea" and has as its object the recovery of the New Testament idea of the laity. That is, *all* believers are *ministers*, and the *pastor's* ministry is to "equip the ministers." Renewal includes an emphasis on commitment to Christ as "Lord," on finding one's own particular ministry, and on the necessity of witness. The basic *method* of accomplishing this is the "small group" idea: small groups in which these ideas can be taught and grasped and, then, through which the ministries can be carried out and one's witness sharpened.

The *Deeper Life,* variously called the "Spirit-filled life," the "abundant life" or the "triumphant life," is an emphasis on the ministry of the Holy Spirit within the life of the believer. The Holy Spirit "indwells" us at conversion (John 14:15-17), but he is frequently an *unappropriated* gift. The Spirit-filled life comes when we grant him the *control* of our lives (a corollary of the "Lordship of Christ"). In Ephesians 5:18, Paul gives us an apt analogy: "And be not drunk with wine, wherein is excess; but be filled with the Spirit" (KJV).

To be filled with wine means to be controlled by it. It affects how we walk and talk and see. So, too, with the "filling" of the Holy Spirit: we allow him to control how we walk and talk and so forth by both a deliberate decision and in a continuing relationship. Only he can produce the Christian life in us. Love, joy, peace, patience, and all the other virtues, are "fruits of the Spirit," not the results of personal effort (Gal. 5:22-23). He is within us to guide, to teach, to lead, and to produce; we are but to yield to him.

The two, "renewal" and the "Spirit-filled life," are not the same in that the latter tends to be primarily inward and individualistic. Renewal tends to link the individualistic with the corporate dimensions of the faith and to emphasize the necessity of the gathered community, the church. At present the two movements are only beginning to meet, but with immense joint potential. The Spirit-filled life can be the "journey inward" step of renewal, and renewal can be the "journey outward" for the deeper life emphasis! Renewal provides a place to go lest the Spirit-filled life become merely a "hot-house" religion, and the Spirit-filled life balances the creative ministry mentality in renewal by stressing those things which "cannot be explained" in terms of human ingenuity and strength, but only "by the Spirit."

The major hurdle between the two movements at this point is a theoretical, yet an important one: *what happens to the "self" in the process of the "journey inward-journey outward"?*

To oversimplify it, the Spirit-filled life movement holds that "self" must be "obliterated"; it must be "crucified" so that it becomes "Christ in you." The renewal movement, on the other (oversimplified) hand, says "self" is "completed" or "made whole" in the process.

Perhaps the difficulty lies in the definition of the "self" which is to be "crucified with Christ." Is it the "essential personality" or is it that "self-centered aspect" in man which chooses "self" as Lord instead of Christ? If it is the "self-centered aspect" (and I think it is), then the issue is resolved. Whether the hurdle is ever crossed, however, the union of the two can at least be a "unity in diversity" *if* they both include the "journey inward" and the "journey outward," the inner life of devotion and the outer life of service.

This is by no means meant to be an exhaustive study. For further reading on the Spirit-filled life, see: *Journey into Fullness, The Christian's Secret of a Happy Life, Life on the Highest Plane,* and *The Key to Triumphant Living.*

On Renewal, see: *The Company of the Committed, The Taste of New Wine, The Emerging Church,* and *No Longer Strangers.* This writer's *Renew My Church* is an attempt to blend the two emphases.

During the course of the week, Dr. Mahoney spoke of the frustrations of trying to "produce" the Christian life in one's own strength. He talked of the ministry of the Holy Spirit in the believer as portrayed in the New Testament: the way the Holy Spirit is the one who is to produce his own fruit; the way Christ had promised the Spirit's presence and power; and the way we are to abide in him, yield to him and follow him. This new idea burst like a bomb: all our sufficiency (and efficiency) in the Christian life is the result of trusting, not trying! Dr. Mahoney then called us to a commitment—not to a cause, but to a person. Many did. And, Heritage Church was never to be the same.

Equally as important was something else which happened during the course of the week. A small group of members approached me after the first few services, asking if Dr. Mahoney and I would come to some of their homes after the remaining services for group meetings to talk more about this idea of yielding to the Appointed Guide. We did so for the balance of the week, probably with more impact than the meetings at the church! These after-service discussion groups became the embryo of the group-life which was to emerge at Heritage and become a part of our new life-style.

Over refreshments in these home meetings after the services, several mentioned that it would be good to do this more—meet and talk about the Christian life. After the services were concluded, the suggestion persisted. Finally, there were enough suggesting it, offering homes and suggesting dates (mostly younger couples) that the Sunday School teacher of the young adults offered her home for such a meeting. The first one was held on Saturday, March 9, 1968. About ten attended, all ages, all members of the church, and all couples.

We decided to meet again the next month, and then the next month. We talked more of the Spirit-filled life and how we could "get a handle" on it. After much searching and talking, I suggested that perhaps the best way was to study books on the themes of renewal and the Spirit-filled life, taking a chapter each time. Agreement was immediate and enthusiastic. And, our "Yokefellow" group was underway!

At the same time, a significant parallel journey also began: that of a large number of Heritage Church members who have never been a part of the "Yokefellow" group, but who have nonetheless been an integral part of the renewal movement. New insights into the nature of the Christian life began to break like stellar explosions in a great many lives in the Heritage Church circle. For most, it started with the Deeper Life Conference, but it both continued and spread. I began an expository series on the book of Acts on Sunday nights immediately following the conference which added fuel to the fire, a series lasting three years and majoring on the ministry of the Holy Spirit to the believer. And, while many of these members were not involved in the group, the same species of growth was taking place among them! God's Spirit is not hemmed in by any *method!*[2]

The Yokefellow group started meeting on a monthly basis, the first Saturday of each month, with a singular objective: to find *authentic Christianity* and our place in it. There was no agenda, no "minutes of the previous meeting," no treasury, no officers, not even a committee! Like Abraham, we "went out, not knowing where we were to go"; but, also like him, we knew we had been called to the *new* and the *better*.

We took the "Yokefellow" name after a few meetings, using the idea of a "common discipline," but not requiring it.

YOKEFELLOWS

PARENTHETICALLY SPEAKING, the "Yokefellow Movement" was started by Elton Trueblood as an encouragement toward disciplined commitment to Christ. it is not a para-church organization but rather, by encouraging better discipleship, it seeks to strengthen existing churches through more committed members. The basic idea of Yokefellows is that of a *mini-*

mum discipline. (An offshoot of the Yokefellow movement, which creates some confusion, has to do with a personal and family therapy program. This is not a part of the original idea nor of our use of the name.) At Heritage, a Yokefellow is one who voluntarily undertakes:

1. *The Discipline of Devotion.* To read a portion of Scripture and to pray each day, preferably in the morning.

2. *The Discipline of Worship.* To share at least once each week in church worship.

3. *The Discipline of Giving.* To share a definite portion of my income in the work of Christ, preferably a tithe.

4. *The Discipline of Study.* To spend time in the reading of Christian books and articles each week.

5. *The Discipline of Ministry.* To discover my ministry and to exercise it faithfully in the power of the Spirit.

6. *The Discipline of Witness.* To share with others, unapologetically, the good news of Christ's ability to save and help.

7. *The Discipline of Fellowship.* To be involved with specific other Christians in an effort of mutual encouragement.

As we frequently say, one cannot "join" Yokefellows; there is nothing to join! One "becomes" a Yokefellow by accepting the disciplines. (See Appendix A.)

We fell into the pattern of my summarizing the chapter for the night and then the group discussing it. In the early days, the first year or so, I confess that it was more my teaching than their discussing. Part of this was by design, but it was mostly through ignorance of good group procedure. God worked through it, however, and perhaps while it was not good group procedure, it was the needed procedure for us at that juncture: we did not know enough to discuss anyhow!

For three years, 1968-1971, the group continued and used this format. Beginning at 8:00 P.M., on the first Saturday of the month, we spent an hour and a half to two hours in studying and discussing the chapter for the night. This was followed by a time of fellowship and we were usually away by 10:30 or 11:00 P.M.

Our first study book was *The Taste of New Wine.* My choice was *The Company of the Committed,* but the choice belonged to them. Then, as now, I sought where they had a "felt need," and suggested a number of possible books, leaving the choice to them. We still follow this procedure. In each case, the group members purchased their own books which we ordered in advance and had available at the meeting. (The choice of the next book was made as we approached the next to the last chapter in the present book. We found, by experience, that most book stores do not carry enough copies for a group of any size and ordering often takes six to eight weeks.)

It was followed by *The Company of the Committed* and then, in succession, by: Elton Trueblood's *The Incendiary Fellowshhp, A Place to Stand,* and *The New Man for Our Time;* Keith Miller's *A Second Touch,* Samuel Shoemaker's *Extraordinary Living for Ordinary Man;* Colin Morris' *Include Me Out;* and Bruce Larson's *Living on the Growing Edge.* Two other books, while not used in the group sessions, which proved immensely helpful were: Douglas Steere's *On Beginning from Within* and Urie Bender's *The Witness.*

These books, taken slowly, month by month and chapter by chapter, introduced the group to "those things necessary to wholeness" in the Christian life. From Keith Miller, we learned about *honesty* and were enabled to quit "faking it" when we didn't have it. From Elton Trueblood, we gained the basic concepts of renewal: that the renewal of Christ's church hinged on *the activation of the laity* in ministry; that unity and fellowship were *prerequisite* to it; that conversion was a call to *commitment to Christ* and to be *a witness;* that love was a *command,* not a suggestion; and that "wholeness" required the inner life of *devotion,* the outer life of *service* and the intellectual life of *rational thought.* Colin Morris vocalized our *frustrations;* Sam Shoemaker gave us some meaningful *practical ideas* on how to "do" the Christian life; and Bruce Larson added the relational aspect of *koinonia* fellowship. Each of these is a part of each of us and we shall always be their debtors: they were pathfinders for us in our pilgrimmage.

We were learning other things, too. For instance, that age groups tend to separate themselves. While the Yokefellow group started with all ages represented, it slowly sifted itself into a young adult group, basically under thirty-five years of age. Over the original three-year span, the older group mostly withdrew. There was no anger, no feeling of being unwanted or anything akin to it. It just happened. A few remained, but only a few. We were to encounter this phenomenon again later in our adult educational program.

AGE GROUPINGS

PARENTHETICALLY SPEAKING, both our Yokefellow groups and our adult Sunday School classes are "wide-open" as to ages; the choice is theirs to make. Yet, we found that they invariably group together in what appeared to be an age-oriented fashion! Upon further investigation, we discovered that age, while evident, was not so much the major factor as was *family patterns*. The presence and the ages of the children were the determining elements: those without children have different schedules (and freedoms) than those who have small children and those with teenagers, etc.

We are now seeing further benefit to this "natural" grouping to the point that we almost view it as necessary to effective group life—especially if the object of the group is to *minister*. For instance, a group of couples or of ladies who want to serve in a ministry group during the days are hindered or helped by common needs: babysitters, children coming home from school, and so forth. The babysitting problem also arises with our retreats. Sharing groups are also aided in that common problems exist according to similar patterns.

Intergenerational groups may be well for dialogue, but ministry groups all but necessitate similar family patterns. We strongly suggest any church's consideration of this factor as they enter renewal groups.

Likewise, we discovered that small groups are viewed with suspicion in existing churches! Previous generations have lived with the aftermath of "church cliques," and that is exactly how they view "groups" and what they most fear about them. In our situation, the apprehension was heightened by the presence of the independent Bible study groups in Annapolis and because some of the people who withdrew from Heritage Church during the "days of disillusionment" were involved in these groups. Consequently, out of valid concern, the Yokefellow group was frequently "visited" by church leaders during the first year or so. Seeing nothing amiss, however, and that their pastor was leading it was sufficient assurance.

Those three years, however slow they seemed to me in terms of spiritual growth, were nonetheless dotted with miracles. Some of the miracles were sudden, unexpected, and exhilarating. Others were "evolving" miracles, but nonetheless exhilarating because they happened to "emerge" rather than "explode."

The most obvious was numerical growth. Over three years, the group grew from the original ten to forty or more packed into the living room of the home where we met. In all, over the three years, some one hundred or so were touched by the group, some being transferred away from Annapolis during the period.

Of course, a number of our younger members are Naval officers and these "passed through" the group a year or two years at a time. Several other members were transferred away by their companies. It was then that we first began to become aware of the wider significance of what we were doing: we began to get reports of Yokefellow groups started by these "missionaries" of ours all across the nation! Since then we have charged these "leavers," at their last meeting with us with the responsibility of doing exactly that.

Who were these "Yokefellows" who gathered over the three years? The answer to that question depends on the focus of the question. *Geographically*, they were from all over! Annapolis is cosmopolitan in makeup, being a Navy town and a bedroom community for Washington and Baltimore, plus having the native Annapolitans. the group was composed primarily of those who had moved to Annapolis and they were from all over: Virginia, the Carolinas, New Jersey, Pennsylvania, the mid-west, Tennessee, Georgia, Oklahoma, Texas, and California. *Vocationally*, they represented the "white collar" group, Annapolis being a clerical and academic city with very little industry. In the group were teachers, professors, insurance salesmen, Naval officers, secretaries, a dentist, a printer, and housewives. *Educationally*, they reflected the city and their work with most, but not all, being college graduates.

Spiritually, however, they were vividly diverse. Looking back, it is easy to place these "groups within the group" into categories.

First, there were those we have come to label the *re-claimed*. These represent the ones who have turned away from the church for one reason or ten. At various times over the three-year period, probably half of the group were those in the "reclamation process." We all well remember one couple who began attending the church *solely* for the sake of their children. They were invited to Yokefellows and came, and kept coming, but were forever expressing cynicism about everything the group held holy. When they later joined the church, they attributed the cause to the Yokefellows who "loved us in spite of ourselves." The significant thing about each of these is that they were "church-born-and-bred" with a rich heritage of faith, yet had all but left the faith entirely, turned away by problems which required a context and atmosphere of acceptance nowhere else available in the church program. They were "reclaimed."

Another segment finding the Yokefellow group attractive were the *lonely*. Especially was this true of the Navy families and of the civilian young couples from other parts of the nation who had been transferred by their companies to the Annapolis area. Many of these are fresh out of school, newly married, and now relocated away from family and friends. Because of this, we now continually stress that Yokefellows must be "instant friends" to all as a part of our discipline.

Another group drawn to Yokefellows were *denominationally-divided couples*. And, in America, these are "legion!" They marry across denominational lines and many times, after a few half-hearted attempts at attending the other's church, they both drop out. But, they feel comfortable coming to *a home*, especially when there are other couples present like themselves. One such couple came to us, he a Lutheran and she a Baptist. They visited our services on a third or fourth round of "trying one another's churches." They did not return to the services—but they did come to Yokefellows when a friend invited them—and they kept coming. They later came into the church, too.

Finally, there were the *seekers*. They were looking. Some were not Christians but wanted to investigate, and the Yokefellow meeting seemed "safer" than a worship service or a crusade. The context of the meetings also allowed for questions to be raised—the very questions which were holding them back. Others were Christians, but they knew there had to be more than just the mechanical going-through-the-motions. This designation best represents the original group which started in 1968 and all along the way more were found.

STARTING A GROUP

PARENTHETICALLY SPEAKING, this experience, confirmed by the years since, allows us to make some *suggestions about starting similar groups* in other places.

1. *Home Setting.* Over and over again, the home setting for such meetings has been reconfirmed. It is more relaxed, more open, and more congenial. It allows those who are fearful of a church service to come with freedom, it is a "neutral" place for denominationally-divided couples, and it lends itself to discussion and fellowship. In choosing such a place, seek a centrally-located one with a large family room. One specific meeting place is a good idea in that it solves the question of "where is the meeting tonight?" We have discovered another value to it in that no one fears if they come that they will have to host the group at their house in return. The host, or "convener," can also invite new people to dinner prior to the meeting and have them stay for, rather than go to, the meeting. More than one Yokefellow started by coming to dinner first!

2. *"Yokefellow" Name.* While the choice of this name for the group was almost accidental, its merit has been repeatedly established. For one, the "minimum discipline" idea of the Yokefellow Movement has been immensely helpful in our encouragement of Christian growth. Another value is that it is a "neutral" name; we often say that "Yokefellows" is not a "Heritage Baptist" group, nor even a "Baptist" group. Consequently, we have always had Catholics, Methodists, and others in the groups. Some of these join the church; some do not, but they become better members of their own churches.

3. *Meeting Format.* The meeting should always have an atmosphere of openness and acceptance, the kind in which anything can be expressed. The leader is important at this point, but the group members are involved, too. It has always been my deliberate attempt to "poke fun" and to compliment various denominations—including Baptists—to set non-members at ease. The format and atmosphere must always be flexible, changing according to who is present. For instance, in the Yokefellow monthly meeting we do not have "prayer sessions," nor do we have "Bible studies." These go on in the smaller groups, but the monthly meeting is designed as an open meeting in which no one should feel ill at ease, especially unbelievers. The evangelistic success of the group has verified this approach. Then, as the Spirit leads, the spiritual level for the night can be reached. A good fisherman knows when to troll and when to pull; "fishers of men" should, too! This open quality allows a person to return—because he is not threatened: a chapter in a book is studied and discussed, but their involvement is entirely voluntary.

4. *Refreshments.* The idea of following the discussion with refreshments, as an *integral part* of the agenda, is also crucial. They are "set at ease" by it and, even if they do not join in the group discussion, they can become "involved" on a one-to-one basis. A conscious effort must be made to make this fellowship period an integral element, however. The group should clearly understand this purpose to it. More than one person has been won or helped in this period that we could not even touch by the study!

5. *"Problem" People.* What do you do with a "problem" person who is always asking questions? (I'm frequently asked that question in conferences!) Remember, the object of your group is to help people, not to have a "good group"! You listen and love, that's what you do! For instance, one night one of our "problem people" asked me if a person had to believe in the Trinity to be a Christian. (This was but one of a thousand similar questions the person raised at every meeting!) My response was to define the Trinitarian idea with the

suggestion that (1) one starts the Christian life with *Christ* and (2) that I would get with them after the meeting in more detail. Remember, winning an argument can lose a convert!

While these ideas may be of little value to groups which are, by design, for "Baptists" or "church members," if a group exists for the purpose of "studying the Christian life," with both believers-in-quest and non-believers, then they will be of help. We can *attest:* they work!

Growing in number across the three years, diverse in background, varied in the stations of their spiritual pilgrimages, they somehow "meshed" and grew together. At the end of three years, as they became more and more in step with each other, there was a *feeling*—a "holy hunch"—that something was going to happen. It was one of those feelings like just before a rain when clouds gather or just before dawn when you know the sun is going to rise; an intuition, a feeling—that God was up to *something!* He was.

Notes

1. While this concept will be dealt with later in the book, it is dealt with in greater detail in my book *The Idea of the Laity.*

2. Early in our faith-experiment, both in and out of the group, we faced and took another decisive step: a position on the "tongues" movement. Annapolis had a number of Bible Study groups, disconnected but at least united in spirit, focused around some of the Deeper Life ideas. In this case, however, there was a tendency towards "tongues." As word spread that the new pastor at Heritage Church was preaching on the Holy Spirit, they began to appear in our services. Having seen the disruption which inevitably follows in the wake of "tonuges," I saw the danger lurking in it. Our new venture of *walking by faith,* under the leadership of the Spirit, could very well be aborted by these who had chosen the lesser way of *walking by sight,* or perhaps more aptly, *walking by signs.* (The New Testament teaches that signs are to follow believers, not the reverse!) We were providentially at Acts 2 in the Sunday night series at that time and I brought two successive messages on "Tongues in the New Testament" and "The Modern Tongues Movement." In them, I took a strong stand against tongues, as does the New Testament. As silently as they appeared, they disappeared and, to this point, no one in our groups or church has become involved.

3. A LONG DAY'S JOURNEY INTO LIGHT

And after six days Jesus took with him Peter and James and John, and led them up a high mountain apart by themselves; and he was transfigured before them (Mark 9:2).

Across those three years from the beginning in the spring of 1968 to the spring of 1971, the Yokefellow group became more and more familiar with the concepts of renewal and the deeper life. At times it seemed unbelievably slow, but at times it was also unbelievably rewarding. The "minimum discipline" was bearing fruit. The group were more in the Word, prayer was becoming meaningful, their love was growing, and they were witnessing. Their journey into Christ-likeness was obviously underway! But, it was slow.

A part of the problem was the redefinition of our *words* which must precede the reorientation of our lives. And that takes time! If it is true that the basic law of learning is repetition, then first having to unlearn means even more repetition! This is especially true with the *vocabulary* of the Christ-life. I soon found that they were not hearing the same words I was speaking!

When I was saying:	They were hearing:
minister	preacher
go deeper	get busier
renewal	revival

fellowship .... church socials
relational .... friendly

But, I also learned to look for something else and I repeatedly saw it happen: a *breakthrough!* Time and time again in our meetings across that three years I saw eyes suddenly widen and with a blink I read their silent shouts: *That's what it means! Now I see it!*

One of those renewal terms was "small groups." Wherever renewal crops out, small groups are present as either *cause* or *effect,* usually both. Every book we studied had something to say about "small groups." And they became interested. While we could have been called a small group at one time, Yokefellows was anything but that by 1971. Month after month saw forty or more crowded into our living room meetingplace. First having grasped the *ideas* of renewal (perhaps it is more accurate to say "grasped by") and now intrigued by the idea of "small groups," it was obvious that this was to be our next step.

Who first introduced the idea? Who knows? As with most of our decisions on this journey together, no one remembers—or really cares. It just seemed evident. The door was suddenly there and it was open. What else could we do but pass through it! It was simply the next *necessary* step. We had seen the value of the group idea in our own lives, especially the deepening aspect which is nowhere else available in the church program. If we were to spread it, then the group had to proliferate itself into *groups.*

There was another reason for it, however, which was unavoidably evident to me: *evangelism.* For at least the last two hundred years, Christianity has carried on its evangelism task with a come-and-hear approach. That is, our methods of evangelism are primarily designed to get people to "come and hear" the gospel. Crusades, church revivals, Sunday School evangelism, bus evangelism, and so forth, all say, "Come and hear." However, we are presently living in a country in which 60 percent of the population (according to the latest figures) will not attend any kind of religious service. *Sixty percent!* This means that a come-and-hear approach begins with a 60 percent audience disadvantage! If we are to reach the majority of *our* population, it will be done *out there* where they are: at work, at play, or wherever. (We do know one place where they will not be: at church!)

In turn, this means that our people must be *taught* to witness. The small group has proven a very effective way of doing this. Also, the home Bible study has proved an effective means of evangelism. While it is still a come-and-hear approach, this feature is greatly offset by the *location*—a home, not a church building. (Leighton Ford, one of the leading proponents of the come-and-hear method, says that the small group is the most promising focal point for evangelistic concern today!)[2] If we were to go deeper-within and wider-without, then the small group idea was the open door.

But, I was frankly apprehensive—probably the only one in the group who was! But, I knew the *dangers* of groups. They can become cliques and they can "go off the deep end!" And even more frankly, I had the normal "98.6" pastor's fear of having groups meeting in "my" church over which I had no control! I knew there was no possible way that I could meet with a number of small groups as I did with the Yokefellow group. They would be "on their own." It was at this point that the idea of the pastor being "the equipper of the saints" (Eph. 4:11-12), beyond the sharing of ideas, became a reality to me. Somehow, they had to be "equipped" to handle themselves *themselves*. But, how? The communal answer was . . . *on a retreat!*

Having settled that the next question was, "What's a retreat?" And, "How do you do it?" I had never been on a retreat, nor had any of them. To be sure, we all had been to "church camp" as children, and on those "retreats" that were either programmed or pointless to a fault; but never a "renewal" retreat, especially like the ones of which we read in our monthly studies.

It was embarrassing to admit to them that I had never led such a retreat. So embarrassing, that I did not tell them! Rather, I asked the group to select some people to "help me in planning it!"[3] Two couples were selected and, along with the teacher of the young couples Sunday School class, we made plans for the retreat. It was decided that we should study (1) group dynamics; (2) various possible small group activities; and (3) what small groups we felt were necessary for us. The date was set for Saturday, May 1, 1971, a one-day retreat. A nearby Catholic retreat house was secured and various members of the group were asked to lead certain portions of the program.

RETREATS

PARENTHETICALLY SPEAKING, even in our "ignorance" God was guiding us. Consequently, a *pattern* for retreats was established by this first retreat from which we have never deviated—with one exception, that of a "time alone" period—during the retreats which have followed the first one. Our basic pattern is:

1. *One-Day Retreats.* While most renewalists advocate the "forty-four hour weekend" retreat, from Friday at 6:00 P.M. until Sunday at 2:00 P.M., we decided on a one-day "crash" approach. We did (and do) this because of the expenses involved with renting a place and with baby-sitting costs which, together, can become prohibitive for a couple. Likewise, we live in a society in which "time" is at a premium. This is not to say that the weekend retreat is not good, but that a one-day approach will work, too.

2. *Self-contained Retreats.* After discussing a number of guest speakers to lead us, we came to the conclusion that a guest would not really know "where we were." So, we decided to use our own Yokefellow participants. Besides, when we use our own, no one can "fake it" as is often the case with outside speakers. We know each other too well for that! Sometime in the future we may invite an outsider to lead a retreat, but to date we have not on any of our retreats.

3. *One-Theme Retreats.* We already had our topic: small groups. But, in our planning we realized that it would be very easy to be too broad. Therefore, we limited ourselves. We have continued to do this. Retreats have the constant problem of either being "too general" so that they are pointless, or of being too fragmented with various topics so that little can be learned and retained. "Be specific" is the rule.

4. *Decisional Retreats.* Our first retreat was held so that we might *do something* as a result of it. And every retreat since has had the same characteristic: each is designed to bring

us to a practical decision. Too many retreats are pointless; good, but pointless. Our retreats, on "discovering gifts" or "the devotional life," or whatever, are planned with a definite objective and with *specific times* for personal and for group decision-making.

5. *One-Book Retreats.* Finally, we decided for this first retreat that we would ask each retreatant to read the book, in this case *Groups Alive-Church Alive, before* the retreat. Our idea was that the brevity of time would not permit "preparing after arrival" (as with Sunday School lessons!). There was another unseen value which emerged, however: that of a common book so that we are all reading in the same vein and sharing the same ideas. This eliminates a great deal of "rabbit-chasing" and deepens the level of the quest.

All of these features can combine to make for a fruitful retreat, brief but deep, and it gives a unique opportunity to actually take forward steps. So much so that, in "charting" their personal and group lives to date, Yokefellows invariably do it in terms of the various retreats serving as the "pegs."

We were ready, then, ready for what can only be termed: *A Long Day's Journey into Light.*

The retreat schedule, beginning at 9:00 A.M., called for a study of group dynamics during the morning and early afternoon. In preparation, those attending were asked to read Clyde Reid's *Groups Alive-Church Alive* which we used as the basis of our study. Various members also read and reported from other books on group dynamics: *Church Meetings That Matter, Spiritual Renewal Through Personal Groups, Group Dynamics in Evangelism,* and *Farewell to the Lonely Crowd.* These reports were "spliced in" at the appropriate chapters in *Groups Alive-Church Alive.*

GROUP DYNAMICS

PARENTHETICALLY SPEAKING, "Group Dynamics" refers to these processes and interactions which all groups have. As Clyde Reid says: "Group dynamics is not something you can have or not have. Group dynamics are. Every group has dynamics."[4] As such, it is not to be confused with "group techniques," that is, room arrangements, "ice breakers" or creative exercises and procedures. "Dynamics" refer to *what is going on* behind the scenes while the group is meeting.

There are two levels of interaction in any group meeting. There is a *program level:* the topic under discussion. There is also a *process* level: the level of feelings and emotions and relationships which goes on despite or in spite of the program. Likewise, there is an observable and predictable *maturation cycle* for any continuing group, from leader-dependence to leader-rejection to independence to independence-rejection to inter-dependence. A group may go through the cycle in an evening, remain at a "step," or even regress, but the cycle is there. And, anyone who would lead or participate in a group, with any success, must be able to understand and to deal with these processes, to read the climate of the meeting, and to analyze the patterns of involvement.

There are also distinquishable "personalities" in a group. Like the "tin god" who always wants his way; the "porcupine" who hides in the group without participating until he suddenly erupts with sharpened bristles; the "white knight" or "Red Cross nurse" who always defends others or their ideas.[5] There is an observable pattern of group flight or engagement with particular ideas and reasons for it. There are ways of handling leadership competition, dominators, frustrators and, especially, cliques.

Many corrective steps are available *to those who know* them. And when the *whole group* knows, it disciplines itself! One can then see the leadership struggle, plot the maturation process and evaluate the meeting in general.[6] A great many problems are solved in advance by establishing a "group contract" regarding the size, purpose, times, leadership styles, and group discipline. That is, all of the members agree on a purpose for the group which, in turn, will often dictate the size of it; starting and ending times are agreed upon; a leadership pattern by one or two or all is established; and disciplines are accepted—to read the book, attend the meetings, be on time, pray daily, and so forth.

All of this, then, is what is meant by group dynamics. The

value is that a group avoids many pitfalls through self-discipline. All of our groups go through this training. Usually a portion of every retreat is given over to a review of it. The value for *a pastor* is that he is able to "free" the group without fear. Consequently, I have never been to any of our small group meetings!

For those who wish to study in the area of group dynamics, the books mentioned in this section are suggested, particularly *Group Alive-Church Alive*.

The latter part of the afternoon was given over to exploring possible small group activities. What kinds of small groups were there? Several group members were asked to share reports from periodicals and books which told of the kinds of groups others were using.

KINDS OF SMALL GROUPS

PARENTHETICALLY SPEAKING, there are many small group possibilities, each with specific characteristics. For instance:

1. *Study Groups.* Study groups are usually of eight to ten members and usually study the Bible or a Christian book. This is similar to our Yokefellow group. These are usually for Christians and for Christian growth.

2. *Prayer Groups.* These groups, which meet regularly for group and/or intercessory prayer, are best kept to six or eight members.

3. *Sharing Groups.* The term "sharing groups" usually conjures up visions of people meeting to talk about their problems and to air their dirty linen publicly. Not so! Rather, they meet and share about their Christian lives, where they are (or are not) and how best to live the Christ-life. They usually follow a theme or a specified topic (witnessing, Bible reading) for the evening and frequently combine Bible study and/or prayer with their sharing. Due to the necessary individual participation, these groups are usually limited to six or so and are usually "closed" to new members until a vacancy occurs.

4. *Evangelistic Groups.* These are groups designed specifically for evangelism. Frequently, they are Bible Study groups, dealing with evangelistic texts or passages and are open to

all who come. (Many groups request members to enlist an unbeliever to attend with them.) Other groups may study a book together, a religious or a secular novel, for evangelistic ideas. Still others use various topics, like threatre groups who attend plays together and discuss them afterward. Always, however, group members understand that their purpose is evangelistic and that they are the "enlisters."

5. *Ministry Groups.* These groups (often called "task groups") are also evangelistic in nature, but they are coupled with service to others and they take place "out there." Thus, they meet at a state hospital, a drug addiction center, or a ghetto playground. Frequently, they focus on specific "target groups" like singles or drug addicts or language groups. The magnitude of the ministry determines the size of the group. Not to be overlooked, however, is a necessary, regular group planning and prayer time in addition to the time spent "on the job."

6. *Support Groups.* A "support group" usually gathers in support of another person or group at various levels of involvement. For instance, a person may be involved in a specialized ministry (drug addiction) about which the group knows nothing; but the group can contribute money, build equipment, and so forth. Or, another person is involved in a "trying" ministry and a group may emerge to pray for the ministry.

7. *Therapy Groups.* This is a specialized, professional ministry and is not for all. Where talent and expertise is available, it can be an effective ministry of outreach and care. Family therapy, personal therapy, group therapy are all exciting Christian options today.

Some of these groups are long-term, some are short-term. Many groups start with a specific time limit, like eight to ten weeks. Others are indefinite in duration. One great value with groups is that they can be laid to rest when they are dead which is not always the case with church organizations. Also, the needs and the nature of the group will determine the frequency of meetings, weekly or every other week or monthly. A definite schedule is to be preferred, however.

For those interested in small group possibilities, we suggest John Casteel's *Spiritual Renewal through Personal Groups;* Ralph Neighbour's *The Touch of the Spirit;* and Elizabeth O'Connor's *Call to Commitment.*

After dinner, we reconvened to discuss "felt needs" for groups among the Yokefellows. A good many were mentioned. Among them were: a group for the parents of small children to study and share ways to effectively rear their children in the Lord; a Bible study group; an intercessory prayer group; a ministry group to work as volunteers at the state hospital; a ministry group to work with welfare boys; another to work with some boys in the church who had no fathers, either by death or divorce; and on and on. We understood that we were only "exploring" the possibilities, thus the range of suggestions was wide. The determining factors, we decided, would be two things. First, we would look for a "match" in "felt needs." That is, the "clue" would be if more than one of us felt the same need. If so, it would be an indication of the Lord being in it. If not, then we would take it as a negative clue. Second, we would not decide immediately. Rather, we would wait until the next meeting to decide, filling the interim with great prayer for direction from Christ.

The 9:00 to 9:00 day, "the Long day's journey," ended with a scheduled hour-long period of "conversational prayer." It was to be their first experience with it, but I somehow sensed that it would be a breakthrough for us. If not, it would at least be a fitting end for the day together.

CONVERSATIONAL PRAYER

PARENTHETICALLY SPEAKING, "Conversational Prayer" is a form of *group prayer* rather than personal prayer. It is different in that it is *natural,* not *usual,* but natural. That is, the usual form of group prayer is either "going around the circle" with each person praying in turn or it is a group gathered, with heads bowed, with various ones praying in turn.

Conversational prayer, however, takes seriously the faith-fact that Christ is *with us,* not "out there." Thus, we "include" him in the group. the prayer takes place, then, as a *conversation* with Christ, a *group* conversation. Imagine a family of grown children gathered for a reunion with their parents. They are seated in the living room. How does it happen? One has a prepared speech and begins. "Dear Father . . ." When he is finished, another begins his speech. Is that the way it happens? I hope not! It should be a group conversation! So, too, conversational prayer.

It also uses ordinary language, rather than "saying your prayers." A person may inject thoughts a number of times. The topic may change, and change again. They may even talk to each other! It understands that prayer is not trying to talk God into something or to persuade him against his will; it is a conversation in which we try to harmonize our wills with the will of God. It is, rather, letting him *talk us* into some things and *persuade us* against our wills! In a very real sense, "conversational prayer" is a redundant expression, like a "tooth dentist." It is *real* prayer!

The most effective prayer groups are those which use conversational prayer. It is more natural and, especially, more personal. For help, see Rosalind Rinker's *Prayer-Conversing with God*.

What happened next cannot adequately be described. Even "breakthrough" seems an inadequate definition. Suffice it to say that 9:00 P.M. passed. And, 10:00 P.M. At 11:00 P.M., I *had* to stop it . . . before we wore out the Lord!

To begin the period of prayer at 8:00 P.M., I asked that all of the chairs be removed and that we gather in a comfortable, widespread circle-of-sorts. I spoke to them briefly of the verse about "where two or three are gathered in my name, I am in the midst." I asked if we believed it, *really* believed it. To emphasize it, I placed a chair in the midst of the group and asked that they make the "faith-assumption" that the Lord was with us and they make the "imagination-assumption" that he was in the chair. "While we pray," I asked, "talk toward the chair." I said that we were going to pray shortly, but that I wanted us to pray in a different way, the way of "conversational prayer." It was a new term to them; their furrowed brows proved it. But, I made no attempt to explain it. Rather, I turned on the overhead projector and let them read some typed transparencies: the first several pages of Rosalind Rinker's *Prayer-Conversing with God*. When they were finished, I prayed first. Others prayed, but "stiffly" at best. I prayed the second time, really to "illustrate" conversational prayer. I prayed something to the effect that it was "strange" that, after having known God for so long, we were so "stiff" and that perhaps we really did not believe, after all, that he was really there. I then "apologized" to him for our behavior! And, that did it.

They really didn't believe he was there! And they said so; not to me, to him! But, they began to believe it. It was unbelievable to believe that they began to believe, but they did. They interrupted one another to talk to him, they talked to one another, and in five-minutes time were veteran conversational pray-ers, simply "including" God in the conversation!

But, even that does not explain what happened. One young man, a Christian for a number of years, startled us all when he said: "Lord, I hate to admit it, but I've never ever spoken to you out loud in all these years." (He hasn't stopped since!) If that was not enough, another said: "Lord, I'm a Yokefellow, a Baptist, and a member of Heritage Church, but I don't know you! And, right here in front of the group, I ask you to come into my life as Lord." And, on and on and on.

The more we have "analyzed" it since, the more evident it is to those of us who were there was that the "breakthrough" was at the point of the . . . *personal*. (It was the same "breakthrough" I had experienced in the crusade prayer meeting in 1967.) Like legions of others, our relationship to Christ had been mechanical and academic. And the effects of it are evident in our "Christian" lives. It is uncanny, yet true, that he can be our personal Savior, but still not be personal! And this is an abiding value of conversational prayer, not as a gimmick, but as a *means* to the personal by providing the accurate context of and for it.

The result for us was a new concept of Christ. We saw him as we never had before, as *personal*. He is *with us!* And that's the significance of the transfiguration, the epigram from which introduces this chapter. It, too, was a conversational prayer experience! Read it!

After six days Jesus took with him Peter and James and John, and led them up a high mountain apart by themselves; *and he was transfigured before them*, and his garments became glistening, intensely white, as no fuller on earth could bleach them. And there appeared to them Elijah with Moses; and they were *talking to Jesus.* (Mark 9:2-4, italics added).

They were "talking with Jesus"; not "praying to," but "talking with." That is *prayer!*

But, a greater truth is the phrase: "and he was transfigured before them." *He* was, not them. They, too, saw him as they never had before. That is the "breakthrough into the personal," the breakthrough *without which* we languish in the church today. For when he is *transfigured,* we are *transformed!*

On the following Sunday morning that transformation became evident. It was a normal Sunday morning in every sense, save one. I preached but did not mention the retreat the day before. Few, if any, even knew there had been one. Until the invitation was given at the end of the sermon for public decisions, that is. Then, one by one, they came—the Yokefellows—down front to where I was standing. Each took my hand and shared his personal breakthrough of the night before. Some twenty-five or thirty came. The choir sang on. The people, usually with their heads bowed for the invitation, began to look up. They were shocked. I mean, *shocked!* When it was over, I started to explain it, but broke down in the telling of it. But they knew; *somehow* they knew; they *all* knew. It was a BREAKTHROUGH!

Notes

1. According to the Associated Press report of *1973 Yearbook of American and Canadian Churches,* April 15, 1973.

2. Leighton Ford, *The Christian Persuader* (New York: Harper and Row, 1966), p. 60.

3. I have since discovered that we were not alone! How does one plan a retreat? Because of this, several of our retreat schedules are included throughout the book. See also: Raymond Magee, ed., *Call to Adventure* (Nashville: Abingdon, 1967) and Larry Richards, *69 Ways to Start a Group and Keep It Growing* (Grand Rapids: Zondervan, 1973).

4. Clyde Reid, Groups Alive-Church Alive (New York: Harper and Row, 1969), p. 46.

5. *Ibid.,* p. 50.

6. See the evaluation form in the author's *The Idea of the Laity,* p. 183.

4. MEANWHILE, BACK AT THE RANCH

"The whole Church throughout Judaea, Galilee and Samaria now enjoyed a period of peace. It became established and as it went forward in reverence for the Lord and in the strengthening presence of the Holy Spirit, continued to grow in numbers" (Acts 9:31, Phillips).

Meanwhile, back at the ranch, there was a church going on. Not everything, *by any means*, centered around the emerging Yokefellow group! There was a church program going on with worship services, Sunday School, church Training, WOMAN'S Missionary Union, and Brotherhood. There was a full slate of committees, our ministry to the Baptist midshipmen, staff meetings, budgets, deacons' meetings, visiting, weddings, and funerals—all of it.

It was during this same time that our church staff meshed. After several misadventures, two persons emerged to join the staff and to become invaluable allies to both the church and to me. First, in 1969, Joan Myers came with us as secretary-office manager. A native Annapolitan, she held a Master's degree in Christian Education and had served in that capacity in two Methodist churches. Disillusioned with the-church-as-is, she left it for a secular position and six months later answered our ad for the position. She subsequently joined the church and her expertise and experience lifted an immense administrative load for me.

Then, in 1970, Willard G. Wild joined us as associate pastor with responsibilities in the areas of religious education and youth. One of our Yokefellow couples had known him in a previous church and knew that he and I were of kindred spirit and perspective. Our interviews with him confirmed it. Several prospects whom we had interviewed were literally "scared away" because of the drift of our church toward the *effective*. (The word *effective* is used in preference to the *new;* they are not necessarily synonymous!) They were "keepers of the records" rather than "equippers of the flock." But, not him. When I warned him that striking new paths might affect his later chances to move to another church—others might be fearful that he would try to "change" them, too, plus the fact that we might fail—he only warmed to the idea!

From staff to structure, renewal was breathing new life into the church; not just the group, but *the total church*. "Renewal" is not "groups," per se. It is an attitude, a perspective. It has to do with the New Testament concept of *ministry*, that *all* of us are called to *our own* ministries and that the church exists *to equip* the members for their ministries by education, inspiration, and the provision of program channels through which those ministries can become the *gifts* to the world that Christ intended. And, inseparably linked to the idea of ministry is the idea of the deeper life. "Ministry" and the "deeper life" are two sides to the same coin; the absence of one devaluates the other!

While perhaps sixty or so of the members were involved in the renewing process in the groups at this time, twice as many more were in the process outside the groups! Most of these had begun their journeys with the Deeper Life Conference in 1968, but they were aided and joined by others through the preaching and teaching programs. Sunday nights, both in the training program and the preaching, were given almost exclusively to this emphasis. During these three years, 1968-1971, I was preaching through the book of Acts, giving emphasis to the unavoidable ministry of the Holy Spirit as the *explanation* of the apostolic church. Having completed that, we started into Paul's epistles, one by one, where we confronted the idea of gifts and ministries over and over again. And, the effects were increasingly evident among the people, those in, *and those not in*, the Yokefellow group.

This is not to say that there was no concern about the group. There was. Frankly, some saw it as a clique. Others saw it as in competition to the Woman's Missionary Union and the Brotherhood, the existing women's and men's groups. And some saw it and did not know what to think about it! It was just *there.* There was no overt opposition, however; just *concern.* And it was *valid* concern! Any church ought to be concerned when a new turn is taken or a new group emerges.

Several things were done to offset this concern. One was that there was no attempt to "hide" it. It was announced from the pulpit, in the bulletin, and in the church paper like any other program and it was made clear that it was *open to all.* Another pacifying element was my personal involvement in it coupled with my equal involvement in everything else. Their "trust" of me, like all human trust, takes both time and experience.

THE PASTOR

PARENTHETICALLY SPEAKING, one of the "keys" to renewal in existing churches, if not the major one, is the involvement of the pastor. He should be the *leader* in it: meeting regularly with the groups, preaching it, teaching it and exemplifying it. However, he must be involved in the *total* church program, seeing that no facet of it, including renewal, receives his exclusive attention.

This does mean, however, a reordering of the pastor's *priorities.* The New Testament assigns the pastor the responsibility of "equipping the saints" (Eph. 4:11-12) and he must take that as seriously as he does literally. He is not there to do it. *for* them, the "star quarterback"; rather, he is to be the "playing coach." In turn, this means he must interpret this "new" concept of the ministry to the people. They were taught, as was he, that his duties were otherwise! Understanding that this is a *process,* rather than an "announcement," greatly aids in the avoidance of many well-intentioned, but just as disastrous, errors! [1]

The greatest aspect in the unifying of Yokefellows and the church was the involvement of the Yokefellows in the regular program of the church. This need was openly discussed at various Yokefellow meetings and, on more than one occasion, I urged them to become involved. Indeed, the group idea is invalid if it does not make better, more involved church members! In turn, the process was aided as church members became involved in Yokefellows. For the first three years, it was "Yokefellows" becoming "church members"; then the tide began to turn—"members" began becoming "Yokefellows"! And a hurdle was crossed.

At present, of the four program directors in the church (Sunday School, Church Training, WMU, and Brotherhood), three are involved in Yokefellows. The chairman of deacons is, along with seven others of the twenty-one deacons. Of the twelve major committees, eight chairmen are Yokefellows. This is likewise the pattern in the Sunday School and the other teaching and training programs. This is the case because a Yokefellow is more than one who attends a monthly meeting. A Yokefellow is one who accepts the "minimum discipline," and only *one point* of it is involvement in a small group. The greater part of the "minimum discipline" has to do with that which makes for better Christians and church members, and, because of the continual group emphasis given to Christ's command to love and to the Biblical emphasis on unity, Yokefellows do not feel, nor have they been characterized, as the "spiritually elite" of the church. Our objective, both in the church and in the groups, is the *renewal* idea: *deeper within-wider without*—with or without groups. I still believe that the small group is the better way to bring it about, but renewal is not limited to the group idea. We saw it emerge outside the group, too! The Spirit of God operates, like the wind, "where *he* wills" (see John 3:8).

That the "deeper-and-wider" concepts of the inner life of the Spirit and the outer life of service were spreading *outside* the group and/or that Yokefellow ideas were spreading *inside* the church began to be evident in the life-style of the *total church*.

A NEW EDUCATIONAL PROGRAM

In 1971, our educational program for adults, particularly the Sunday School program, began to feel and exhibit the effects of the renewal emphasis. It focused on both the *methods* and the *purpose* of adult education. Up until then we had operated along traditional lines with age-graded departments; small, separate men's and women's classes; and using standard literature. Then, however, new ideas began to surface. They came from several sources.

One issued from the academic mileau of Annapolis itself. A large number of our adults are related to the Naval Academy and other area colleges. Likewise, as a later survey revealed, some 78 percent of our adults held college degrees and 53 percent held graduate degrees. Their focus was on *methods*. "Why," they asked, "have small classes"? (They taught or took courses with forty or more in class.) "Why separate classes for men and women?" (Educationally, it is not done from grade school to graduate school.) And, more pointedly, they asked, "Why *age* grading?" (The new commuter college idea, with its emphasis on night classes for working adults, has revealed the workability of cross-generational classes.)

Another source was our young adult department, Adult I. They focused on *methods*, too. They asked permission to experiment for one year. They wanted (1) to have a "mixed" class offered in addition to the men's and the ladies classes; and (2) to do away with "opening exercises," substituting a "coffee time" in its place along with a mimeographed news sheet to compensate for the lack of an announcement period. Knowing that it wouldn't work, I granted permission to prove the point. In six months, the separate classes were nonexistent, the mixed class grew, and the coffee time was greatly enjoyed! So much so, that Adult II asked to do the same! That is, *half* of Adult II did. The other half somehow feared that it would be either disloyal or sin, or both, to do it. Agreement was reached among them, however, by having a coffee time *every other* Sunday and a trial mixed class. It worked there, too! But, not without tension.

The third source came from the Yokefellows. Their focus was *functional*. As they began to take seriously the Bible and the new life they were discovering, they began to be very aware of their biblical illiteracy. It was especially evident when they began to serve and to witness. They did not quite know the source of the problem, but they knew they had been in Sunday School most of their lives with somehow not learning very much. My response to their questions was: "I thought you'd never ask!" For a long time I had the growing conviction that *if* the purpose of Sunday School is to *educate*, particularly in the Bible, and *if* the purpose of the church is to *equip* people for their ministries, then we were (heaven forbid!) doing it *wrong*. By that, I mean that when a ministerial student goes to seminary to study the Bible, he does not study it as we do in Sunday School: a passage here, a passage there. Rather, it is Old Testament Survey, New Testament Survey, and so forth. Additionally, in seminary they realize that "basic equipment" for service requires a study of theology, ethics, Christian history, and the like. If this is the *proper way* to train the "professional," *why not the laity?* I whispered it, but they said it!

As these ideas began to cluster and to confuse, I had to face them. They would not go away. My first concern was the *functional* and I admitted the validity of survey course approach. Another concern was *methods* and I wrestled long with these proposed changes. My conclusion shocked *me!* I concluded that these methodological changes were being suggested by *loyal* members who were *adults*, not rambunctious teenagers, and many of them were *professional* educators. I, also, concluded that, as pastor, I was responsible for providing programs to equip . . . *them;* it was *their* education, not mine. I shared these conclusions with Willard and Joan. They agreed. We shared them with the deacons and church leaders, and the outgrowth of it was the appointment of an Adult Education Study Committee of twenty-four members, representing all age and attitude groups and chaired by one of our most creative men, to study and make recommendations to the church. The result was a restructuring and a reorientation of our adult educational program.[2] *And, renewal was evident!* Their primary thrust was *functional:* Christian education should equip Christians to serve Christ in the world in the power of the Spirit. Their secondary thrust was *structural:* what is the *best* way to do it? They answered both confidently and the church responded affirmatively. And it has worked for us.

We now have three adult divisions which are designated, without age-grading, as Young Adults, Median Adults, and Senior Adults; and each member chooses where he or she best fits. They invariably group in similar age clusters, but the major factor seems to be family patterns and ages of the children. All classes are mixed (We make the careful distinction between "mixed" and "couples" classes; not all adults are married!) except for the Senior Adults who wanted separate classes as they had had most of their lives. Our response was: it is *their* education. Also, each division has but one class. This makes a large class, but it avoids any "popularity contest" among teachers, a very real problem.

This largeness was offset by another factor. The Adult Education Study Committee (AESC) also recommended a parallel program on Sunday morning: that of a "Christian Basics" series of survey courses. Consequently, two "trial" courses were tried to see if there was interest in such and to work out the "bugs." They were successful and we structured the program. It is a two-year cycle of courses, each on a thirteen-week, quarterly basis, except for the summer quarter (July, August, September) when so many are away on vacation.

	Year One	
FIRST QUARTER	SECOND QUARTER	THIRD QUARTER
(Oct.-Dec.)	(Jan.-Mar.)	(Apr.-June)
O. T. History	*Life of Christ*	*Life of Paul*
	Year Two	
Church history	*Christian Ethics*	*Doctrine*

This cycle is repeated every two years to incorporate new members and for the sake of those who might be teaching elsewhere in the program during one cycle. The regular Sunday School program for adults runs parallel to this so that an option is available to all. For our regular program we utilize curriculum materials from the Church Services and Materials Division of the Baptist Sunday School Board, Nashville, Tennessee. In the summer quarter, all return to their regular classes. Future courses for those completing the two year cycle will grow out of the cycle itself and will be chosen by the classes, such as the Prophets, the Prison Epistles, the Reformation, and so forth. (See Appendix B for the curriculum of the "Christian Basics" Series.) An "Adult Education Committee" is appointed annually to receive suggestions and to make further recommendations to the staff as to need and interest. For youth and down we continue to follow grouping and grading structures recommended by the Baptist Sunday School Board. And we make use of curriculum materials from the Board.

A NEW SUNDAY NIGHT APPROACH

Near the end of the Sunday night preaching series on Acts in 1971, we began to notice a drop in attendance, a decline which continued for some time. Several factors were contributing to it. One was fear. Being downtown, surrounded by dark streets and all, plus a number of reported muggings in the area, night attendance was effected, especially among the women. Our Church Training program was not helping the situation either as the people were dissatisfied with the suggested programs and materials. And, finally, there was a monotonous sameness about the evening service itself. Due to our study of Acts, the format for three years had been unchanged. We had already faced the fact that Sunday night had ceased to be the "evangelistic hour" it had been in the fifties, at least *for us*. A change was needed (which is the only time for change, when it is *needed*); why not a *renewal* change?

Willard and I discussed it at some length, coming to several conclusions: (1) Sunday night was for Christians; (2) What we were doing was too much the same; (3) We should use it to equip and to inspire. Our one basic conclusion, however, as we began to think creatively about moving toward the *effective* was that *Sunday is the first day of the week*. Sound simple? It isn't! Most of us operate on the unexamined premise that it is the *end* of a week, the Old Testament idea. Thus, we spend all week *getting ready* for next Sunday. (Read any church newsletter if you need verification.) And many times, when Sunday does not come up to our expectations, we leave the church on Sunday night . . . *disappointed*. What a way to start a week! Why not send them out excited about the possibilities of the week before them? Thus, we had our *functional* premises for Sunday night: to equip and to excite. We developed some ideas and shared them with the deacons, suggesting that we experiment during the summer and fall of 1971. They heartily endorsed the idea of experiment and, after several "trial runs," a new format emerged.

Church Training. For the Church Training hour we developed a series of month-long seminars designed to equip people both to understand their world and how to minister in it. To secure their points of need, we distribute survey forms for their suggestions and discuss these with the Adult Education Committee.[3] Over the past several years, we have had such seminars as: Christian Black Studies, The Christian and Political Structures, The Christian Family, The Devotional Life, The Principles of Church Renewal, Witnessing, Transactional Analysis *(I'm O.K., You're O.K.)*, The Cults, Teaching Methods, and The Ministry of the Holy Spirit.

Evening Worship. For the evening worship hour, we established a "theme" for each Sunday night of the month, all designed to inspire and to send them out into the week "proud to be a Christian." On the first Sunday night, we have baptismal services and I preach sermons designed to express that "God is alive and well on the planet earth." The second Sunday night of each month is a *Youth Service*, led entirely by the teenagers. This is not a "junior-adult service," however, with singing led by a teenager and a sermon by a "youth pastor." They utilize music, art, drama—almost a performance!

YOUTH RENEWAL

PARENTHETICALLY SPEAKING, this monthly Youth Service reflects another move toward renewal in education. Willard Wild developed this concept, which he calls "learning-doing," as an outgrowth of his own renewal pilgrimage. As the Church Training program for youth began to wane, along with the other Sunday night emphases, he was searching, too. The result was the conversion of the Youth Training Program hour into a preparation time for the monthly Youth Service! But, it was to be far more than a performance staged for the adults each month. He wanted to use it to *train* and *equip*. Consequently, each program has a theme, usually biblical, and the teenagers are called upon to develop it into a program.

One of the programs was on the prodigal son passage. Rather than merely study it, lecture-style, he asked them to rewrite the story in a contemporary setting; in fact, in Annapolis! And, then to present it to the adults. But, how? Their decision was to make a film of it. Thus, the "prodigal son" was seen leaving home, throwing his golf clubs and suitcase into the back of his sports car, and venturing forth to . . . Baltimore! A study of the crucifixion led to a musical program. Another program centered around the four stained-glass windows in our sanctuary (Christmas, Good Friday, Easter, Pentecost), presented as a drama with an "on-the-spot report" of each by a biblical character. In every case, the learning is in the doing!

The third Sunday night is a *Lay-Led Service*. The object of this service is two-fold: to give the laity a medium of public witness and to encourage other lay men and women to do so. Here, again, it is not an "amateur hour imitation" of the kind of service the pastor leads. Rather, it takes the form of an *interview* of one or more of the laity, sometimes by the pastor, sometimes by the laity, and around a *particular theme*. For instance, our first lay-led service was an interview by me of a junior high biology teacher on "A Teacher's View of Teens." The pulpit was removed and replaced by two chairs. While I asked and he answered questions about the school system, the attitudes of youth, etc., I was also able to ask him about his own Christian life. This accomplished two things: he was able to inform the teens that he was a Christian and how he became one; and, he inspired other adults to say "I'm a Christian" *out loud!*

LAY SPEAKERS

PARENTHETICALLY SPEAKING, particular care is given in the selection of the ones who lead or participate in the Lay-Led Service each month. That is, we seek the "quiet" ones, persons with whom the majority of the people can identify. If we chose the more articulate, polished public speakers, it could be more *discouraging* than encouraging to the ordinary lay person. They could say, "If I was as educated, as smooth, as articulate, as he is, then I could do that, too; but I am not, therefore, I cannot!" Consequently, we choose those who are not the "regular" church leaders.

Other services have focused around young families, the world of daily work, and so on. Our deacon ordination services are included in the Lay-Led series, also. A recent Father's Day was a "third Sunday" and I interviewed three fathers on the "Changing Role of *Christian* Fatherhood" by using one father with small children, one with teenagers, and one with grandchildren. The fourth Sunday night of the month is given to religious films, choir presentations, etc., again designed to inspire and excite.

The Sunday morning and evening approaches are, perhaps, the more obvious effects of the renewal perspective in the church-at-large, as opposed to the Yokefellow groups, but they are not the limit to it. It became more and more evident, in a myriad of ways, that the *deeper within-wider without* objective was the emerging life-style of the total church.

ANNUAL PROGRAM

Renewal reflected its widening circle of influence in our annual program of special events, also. Our "January Bible Study" became more than a perfunctory necessity. We sought to make it an integral part of the equipping process by making it a time of *practical* suggestion, as opposed to *theoretical* study. We already knew more than we were doing; we needed help with doing what we already knew! In the years when the suggested book appears to be more theoretical, we provide an alternative. This usually takes the form of a Laymen's Theological Seminar or a Deeper Life emphasis. During this period, then, we had studies in "The Present and Future of the Church," a seminar led by Dr. Ralph Neighbour on "Contemporary Evangelism" and a second Deeper Life emphasis led by Dr. James Mahoney.[4]

Another special event had to do with the role of the *family* in renewal. If the Christian faith does not help in the family circle, then it is elsewhere invalidated, too. Again, however, our focus was and is on the practical: *how?* How do we teach our children about the things of God? How do we pray together? How does Christ relate to us in our ever-changing roles as mates, parents of small children, teenagers, etc.? How does one *do* the Christian life at home? What practical and biblical suggestions are there to be made? Thus, we have an annual weekend "Family Life Conference" each spring with a noted authority in the field, such as Dr. John Drakeford, Dr. T. B. Maston, or Harry Hollis. Additionally, we have an annual Family Retreat over the Labor Day Weekend. The church rents the Maryland WMU camp, Camp Wo-Me-To, for the Friday through Monday period and we spend it together as families. However, we do not study about the family during the weekend; our object is to provide a time and a place *to be families*. Therefore, the schedule is kept to an absolute minimum with devotional periods in the morning and the evening, the balance of the time being free for the families to be together! In our hurry-up world just the provision of an occasion to be together becomes a ministry!

COLLEGE STUDENTS

The church's ministry to the Baptist midshipmen at the United States Naval Academy in Annapolis was initiated in 1904, but in the main it was the provision of Sunday School and worship services. There was, however, a growing realization that *real ministry* had to entail more than that. A few families befriended certain mids and welcomed them into their homes, but it was by no means the norm. In 1970, we started an "Adopt-a-Mid" program whereby each incoming Baptist "plebe" (freshman) was "adopted" by a church family. We were beginning to see that two hours on Sunday morning was not adequate for any significant Christian influence upon their lives. (Midshipmen, due to the vigorous Academy program, are not permitted out on Sunday or Wednesday nights; therefore, our program is Sunday morning only.) Each year since we have simply added new plebes until now each of the Baptist mids is related to some family in the church. To aid in this, we moved our Sunday morning service from 11:00 A.M. to 10:30 A.M., allowing a half-hour for after-service "fellowship" before they have to be back for "noon formation." Then, twice each month, we provide refreshments in the fellowship hall following the service to give a better context for it. We also provide coffee and doughnuts before both Sunday School and worship for the late-risers. This gives us *specific* times to meet, in addition to the time spent at church and in their homes.

The renewal emphasis of small groups entered into it, also. Our on-campus ministry was limited to personal visits without any group meetings led by outsiders being allowed. Seeing the effectiveness of lay-led groups at work in Yokefellows, we presented the idea of training the mids to lead their own groups. At first apprehensive of it, the idea caught on and some of the Yokefellows began to train leaders in how to start groups and about small group techniques. Again, the renewal ideas were operative *outside* the group in the total church.

DEACON SELECTION

Like eleven out of ten Baptist churches, a major index for deacon selection at Heritage Church was *business ability;* not the *only* index, by any means, but at least a major one. It was referred to as "the Board" with the connotation of "Board of Directors." In 1967, however, after being (somehow!) without a Church Constitution, a committee of deacons was appointed to write one for adoption by the church. In the writing of it, they wrestled long with the section of "Deacons, Duties of," and finally decided that it was a *spiritual* office, not a business one! Thus, they committed the "business" to committees and decided to give themselves to the "spiritual leadership of the congregation"! (Lest any attribute this decision to pastoral "guidance" or "suggestion," it needs to be said that this was all done during a period of 1967 when the church was without a pastor!) Now, the only "business" considered by the deacons is that for which no committee is responsible or any item which might effect the spiritual life and fellowship of the congregation.

They gave themselves to a ministry of "family care." (See Appendix D.) But, it was not as easy as they had thought! They were not equipped to do it and, by 1971, it was more than obvious. We responded in two ways. First, a new *index* for deacon selection began to emerge and it was finally vocalized in the thought that a deacon should be one to whom others already look for spiritual leadership. Thus, "ordination" was not so much the "making of a deacon" as it was the *official recognition and confirmation* of what the congregation had already done! Second, a twenty-minute "training session" was incorporated into the agenda of the monthly meeting. During this time, the staff informs them of the total program (and its objectives) to make them *knowledgeable* leaders, and teaches them how to visit in the home or hospital, how to deal with a critic, etc., to make them *effective* leaders.

DEACONS AND RENEWAL

PARENTHETICALLY SPEAKING, at this point, I became very aware of an oversight on my part, an error in the strategy of renewal. had I to do it over again, I would start the renewal process with church leaders, particularly the deacons. They are the ones already looked to for spiritual leadership and the regular monthly meeting is an ideal opportunity for teaching them. One would do well to start there by including training sessions and by "deacon retreats" along the themes of the deeper life and the lay ministry.

Our present meeting format is as follows:

        8:00-8:10—Devotions
        8:10-8:30—Training Session
        8:30-8:35—Reading of the Minutes
        8:35-8:45—Family Care Reports [5]
        8:45-   —Business

While we are still struggling in making the transition, we are farther along than we once were. And, that's "renewal"—it is a *process*.

This is by no means a full report on the penetration of the *deeper within-wider without* ideas into the *total* church life, but it is sufficient to illustrate its growth and development. All of it emphasizes that renewal is a *process* and that it is not limited to "groups," though the group idea seems the more effective way of accomplishing it. Renewal is first of all an *attitude*, a *perspective* about the role of the church and the purpose of the Christian life: "The equipping of the saints for the work of the ministry" (Eph. 4:11-12).

OUR NEW LOCATION

This was our "acid test." In 1970, after making overtures for several years, the State of Maryland "laid claim" on our property for the expansion of the state government facilities in Annapolis, Maryland's capital city. Located adjacent to the state capitol building and the governor's mansion, and surrounded by existing government buildings, we were prime contenders for their "offer." When it came, I was frankly afraid. No, I was . . . *scared stiff!* Were we *spiritually* ready for it? There was no doubt about it, it would be a "gift from God" to move. We were hemmed in by buildings; no daytime parking was available, thereby limiting our weekday program possibilities; and our facilities were old and deteriorating. Yes, it would be a "gift" . . . except for the fact that it would require selling the building in which many of them had grown up, been converted, baptized, married, and from which loved ones had been buried! It would require both relocating and *renaming* the church, since we had a "street" name: *College Avenue.* Fortunately, finances would not be a problem: our buildings were paid for and the state offered us $975,000 for our property which, with investment during the process, would accrue to well over $1,000,000!

Without going into the full details of how we purchased our new ten-acre site, renamed ourselves "Heritage Baptist Church" and constructed a new million-dollar complex, debt-free, there are two clues to the significance of it.

First, the Dedication Litany, read responsively on Dedication Day, March 5, 1972, reflects the emerging presence of *renewal* among us. Notice carefully the *purposes* for which the building was dedicated.

As a MEETINGHOUSE for the study and the proclamation of the Word to children and youth, to collegians and midshipmen, to adults and to families . . .
PEOPLE: We dedicate this House.
As a HEADQUARTERS for the company of believers, known collectively as the Heritage Baptist Church, and from which the gathered group shall scatter to become as holy seed in the Annapolis fields . . .
PEOPLE: We dedicate this House.
As a MEMORIAL to our College Avenue past, acknowledging our debt to a great cloud of witnesses now above us, and yet in spirit with us . . .
PEOPLE: We dedicate this House.
As a SERVICE CENTER to our community, providing a place of refreshment for the bodies, minds, and spirits of those to whom it is our responsible privilege to minister in the name of Christ our Lord . . .
PEOPLE: We dedicate this House.
As a SANCTUARY, a place where prayer is wont to be made, baptisms

and communion observed, tithes and offerings given, hymns sung and anthems heard, a place where we our Savior meet . . .
PEOPLE: We dedicate this House.
In the NAME of, and for the GLORY of, and by the GRACE of God the Father, God the Son, and God the Holy Spirit . . .
PEOPLE: We dedicate this House.

Second, the presence of *koinonia*, a basic element in the life-style of renewal (indeed, the *verifying* factor of it if John 13:35 is to be taken seriously), was unmistakeably visible. Suffice it to say that we sold the old building to be demolished, decided on a new site, renamed the congregation, built the building—without a breech of fellowship!

In 1972, I knew we were "home free" in renewal! We had not "arrived," but the BREAKTHROUGH had been made. There was an *attitude* there which, having passed the "acid test," said that road to renewal was at least open and clear to the willing. In terms of the title of Wallace Fisher's intriguing book, *From Tradition to Mission*, we were . . . *halfway!*

When put together, our "report" says something extremely significant and encouraging. It says that *renewal can take place in an existing church!*

Notes

1. See the writer's *The Idea of the Laity,* Chapter 3, "The Ministry: Torchbearer or Lamplighter?"
2. See *The Idea of the Laity,* Chapter 5, "Christian Education—to Equip or Entertain?"
3. See Appendix C for a sample form.
4. This second conference with Dr. Mahoney provided the context for the development of his book, *Journey into Fullness.*
5. Each of our twenty-one deacons is assigned a certain number of families for whom they are responsible to serve as a "pastor." Also, four deacons serve as a "new member" committee, taking new members under their care as they join. The Baptist Sunday School Board offers an excellent set of records on Deacon Family Ministries. These can be purchased at any Baptist Book Store. See Appendix D for a sample Deacon's "Calling Card."

5. ONE STEP FORWARD, TWO STEPS BACK

On the evening of that day, the first day of the week, the doors being shut where the disciples were, for fear of the Jews, Jesus came and stood among them (John 20:19).

Nearly all Yokefellows "date" their pilgrimages by the Manresa Retreat. It was a "breakthrough" in every way, but especially in the realm of their personal relationships with Christ. There was to be no turning back from now on; there could not be. It was an experience we could not explain, but it was more than "an experience" as that expression is usually interpreted. It was a *commitment*, both to the *Person* and to the *pursuit* . . . of renewal.

A commitment! Once Aileen and I were on a plane which caught on fire and had to make an emergency landing. We had just taken off when the plane made a sudden lurch, banked around, and began to descend. Almost as quickly as we had taken off, we were back on the runway with fire trucks rushing to meet us. We discovered later that the plane had actually caught on fire while we were still on the runway in the process of taking off! But, the plane had reached such a speed, and had passed a point on the runway where we had to go on. The airline people said, "The pilot had *committed* himself" when that speed and point was passed and, when he *committed* us to taking off, we had no choice. It was the point of no return. That was the Manresa Retreat for the yokefellows: *commitment!* The deeper and the wider were unavoid-

63

able now. and. a major facet of it was small groups.

It was evident at the next regular meeting of Yokefellows. Several groups had already started: a weekly men's prayer group and a group of parents with small children who wanted to study and pray together every other week about how to be better parents. As we discussed the retreat. particularly the small groups we wished to launch. several possibilities emerged into reality. A number of the ladies decided to become involved in an existing WMU mission action group. ministering one day each week to a women's ward at nearby Crownsville State Hospital. (Renewal does not necessarily mean the creation of new groups. Many times it reflects itself through *existing* programs and ministries.) Then. some of the ladies in the group decided to start a "Ladies Day Out" ministry by once a month providing a nursery for mothers who wished to "get away" for a few hours. They envisioned this as an evangelistic tool. being able to invite their friends to be with them for an informal time of shopping or dinner and of . . . witnessing! On the other three Tuesdays of the month. they decided to have a Bible study to which they could "reinvite" these new friends. Two other couples formed a "seeking group." trying to work through some theological problems they had. I had personally decided to start a "career-singles" group (we had two in the Yokefellow). using the group members as "self-leaders." A few met with me and they launched both a Sunday morning and Thursday night Bible study. using the week-night meeting for evangelism—plus. a couple of other Bible study groups from among the Yokefellows seemed on the verge of becoming a reality! We were *on the way!*

Another major decision made that night was to retain the monthly meeting of Yokefellows: the *groups* needed the *group*. I had left this decision with them. but with great apprehension. I wanted very much to continue the meeting for several reasons. The first was purely selfish: I needed the group! Then. I knew that they needed each other and. hopefully. me! But. I also saw the value of it in terms of coordination. that of a time and a place where *all* the groups came together. Strangely enough. they expressed these very ideas! I was exuberant!

COORDINATION OF GROUPS

PARENTHETICALLY SPEAKING, it is still our pattern to use the monthly Yokefellow meeting as the "hub" of our group activities. the small groups, called "Yoke" groups, meet weekly or every other week as they choose to do so. Graphically, it appears as:

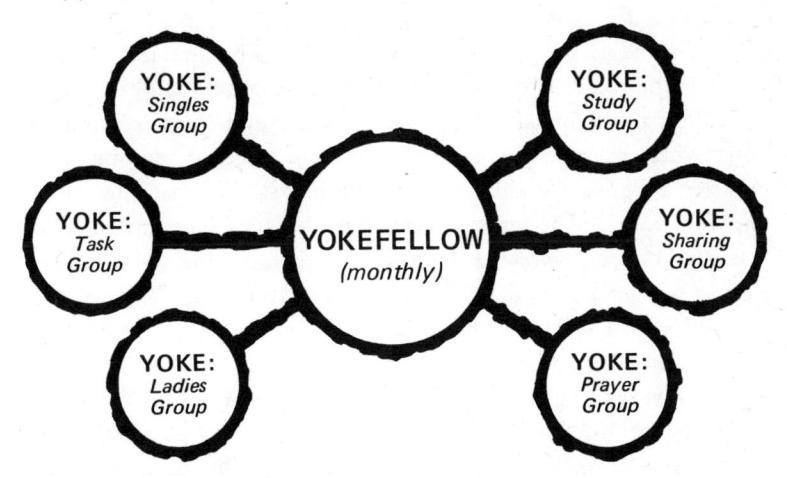

```
    YOKE:                    YOKE:
   Singles                   Study
    Group                    Group

YOKE:                                      YOKE:
 Task         YOKEFELLOW                  Sharing
 Group         (monthly)                   Group

    YOKE:                    YOKE:
   Ladies                   Prayer
    Group                    Group
```

The value of this pattern is two-fold. First, it allows the pastor to "relate" to all of the groups without attending each one: he meets with them in the monthly group. The "opening question" of each monthly meeting is, "What's going on in the Yoke groups?" and reports are made of their activities. This keeps both the pastor and the group members not involved in that particular group informed and, in a sense, *involved.* We stress that, though we meet separately, we are each *involved* in *all* of the groups. Second, it serves to *coordinate* the many small groups. To try to do so without this "coming together" each month would be an administrative nightmare.

Then, too, the idea of the whole group studying one book gives a sense of unity to it as a movement. While our ministries vary, our study is mutual and we are "thinking on" the same things *together.*

We strongly suggest this kind of pattern to any who venture into small group ministries.

As the weeks and months began to pass, however, disappointment in the groups began to emerge. It was not "working" as well as we had anticipated. At first, we attributed it to the summer months. The retreat had been in May and we tried to start the small groups in the summer when so many were taking vacations and weekend trips. But, when summer was over, there was no question about it. We had a *problem!*

First, some of the groups began to "fold." The "parents group" was the first to go. After six or eight meetings, they had exhausted both their problems and their solutions! Several couples dropped out, several moved away and the others wanted to regroup with another purpose for the group; a "Bible study," perhaps, or a "prayer group." The "men's group" got off to a bad start. It had actually started *before* the Manresa Retreat, getting its initiation from what I suspected as the thought that neither Yokefellows nor I were sufficiently *spiritual,* that is, *did not use the proper cliche's.* (We deliberately sought to avoid the "churchy" atmosphere in the Yokefellow meetings, trying to provide a context in which seekers would be comfortable. Some have thought this to be unspiritual while, in fact, we were not trying to *appease* Christians so much as to *appeal* to seekers.) But, whatever the motivation, it lacked a *purpose.* It floundered about, first as a study group, then a prayer group, then it sought a mission. They decided on a ministry to boys and investigated the possibility of a Royal Ambassador program. Excitement grew about it but when no one would assume responsibility, it died, too, and the group finally folded. The "seekers group" met successfully for awhile, but it also died when one couple moved some distance away from the other.

Several other "planned" groups never started. They were talked about, Bible studies and prayer groups, along with several ministry groups, but nothing came of them. I refused to "start" them, wanting the initiative to come from the Yokefellows themselves. I did, however, "start" a career-singles group from among those already in the church. I called them together, but finding no leaders, was forced to put the leadership responsibility on them. But, no inner leadership emerged. They "met" for nearly nine months on Sunday mornings, but that was all: they just *met.*

All of this led to my personal disappointment, as well as that of the whole group. And for the first time since 1967, I felt a hint of disillusionment. Nothing, however, disappointed me as much as the obvious fact that the group did not want to *minister*. All of the groups were in-grown, focused on themselves. I had envisioned the groups emerging around tasks and ministries. In fact, I had called some really exciting possibilities to their attention at the retreat and in the subsequent monthly meetings. There was a large welfare housing complex close to the church, filled with poverty and with an observable absence of men in the homes. I suggested a ministry to the boys, perhaps a recreational program, with an evangelistic thrust; a ministry to the mothers, focusing on how to sew, to cook, to shop, etc., helping them on an economic level and adding the spiritual to it. I, also, wanted to see a ministry to alcoholics. But, no takers! I talked to the group about the fallacy of "sitting around examining one another's halos," but it only added to their grief. The group was really afraid to "mix it" with the world! And guilt was added to our grief.

Fall, winter, spring, and summer passed; a full year since Manresa. By then the failure was too obvious to avoid any more. Embarrassment or guilt, or whatever, at first would not permit any of us to mention it aloud and, when we did, it was on the one-to-one basis of personal conversation. Happily, however, the mutual question was the right one: *Why?* If we had bogged down with *how,* we would simply have been more enthusiastic in our failure. Or, if the question had been *what* we would have but added variety to our failure. But, it was *why*. Why had we failed? And, because that was the question raised, we began to *pray*. You see, *how* and *what* don't pray; they *do! Why* prays. It prays because it does not know *why* or *how* or *what*; it *has* to pray! Long afterward, when we were able to talk about it, the unity of our prayers, unknown at the time, was unbelievable—and unmistakably of the Spirit.

In private conversations and small gatherings, we began to sort out some reasons and explanations. We were greatly aided by a study of "gifts and ministries" which was (providentially) in one of the books we were studying at the time. It led many of us to do personal Bible study about it. By the summer of 1972, more than a year after Manresa, several reasons for our failure finally became clear, clear enough that we already knew the topic of our *next* retreat: *gifts* and *ministries!* We scheduled it for October 7, 1972, at Pine Lane Retreat Center, another Catholic retreat house on the outskirts of Annapolis.

THE NEED FOR RETREAT CENTERS

PARENTHETICALLY SPEAKING, the Roman Catholics are far ahead of all of us in the provision of retreat houses for such meetings. The future will indicate, however, that "retreat houses" will become necessary to the on-going of the church as church buildings are to us today!

The Catholics are ahead of us (or, perhaps, are leading us) in that these retreat houses were once used only by priests and nuns for their required annual retreats. Now, they have simply opened them to the public! And, these are constantly filled so that reservations must be made far in advance. This is a bad feature in that, as we have found, retreats are usually needed "now," just as a BREAKTHROUGH occurs! That is the time to do it, with perhaps a month for planning, yet it is all but impossible to get such a place on a month's notice. The slack in retreat places has been taken up in part by summer camps (YMCA, etc.) and independent retreat houses such as the Yokefellow Retreat centers, Laity Lodge, and others. But, even these are insufficient to handle the need now, let alone the future needs.

The answer lies, to some degree, in the denominations winterizing their present camps for year-round use and, in some cases, building new retreat centers. One church in my knowledge recently built motel-like accommodations into their new educational building for retreats! Several churches now have their own retreat centers and, while this would be financially impossible for most churches, several churches going together could do it. Old waterfront or wooded estates can easily be adapted. Another unexplored avenue is that of motels located on once-busy highways, but now by-passed by interstate highways. In many cases, these already have restaurant and swimming facilities.

Whatever the answer, however, the need is there. The denominations *must* come through, and the churches as well—lest it become too evident who exists to support whom! And, for laymen of means, there could be no more needed investment in the kingdom of God than the provision of retreat centers. It is a must!

While the pattern of failure was not yet clear, one element of it that we began to see was *that we had been thinking in terms of "groups" rather than "gifts"!*

GIFTS AND MINISTRIES

PARENTHETICALLY SPEAKING, the Bible teaches that *all* believers have "gifts" or "ministries"—each has his or her own "calling." The Christian community has arbitrarily limited the idea of a "call" to the professional ministry: pastors, missionaries, evangelists, etc. And wrongly so! The Bible insists that all are "called." The various lists of gifts in the New Testament include ministries and functions which cannot be limited to pastors alone. In the Epistle to the Romans (and remember to whom he is writing: the people, not the pastor!) Paul says:

> For as in one body we have many members, and all the members do not have the same function, so we though many, are one body in Christ, and individually members one of another. Having gifts that differ according to the grace given to us, let us use them: if prophecy, in proportion to our faith; if service, in our serving; he who teaches, in his teaching; he who exhorts, in his exhortation; he who contributes, in liberality; he who gives aid, with zeal; he who does acts of mercy, with cheerfulness" (Rom. 12:4-8).

Again, in 1 Corinthians, written to another group of Christians in another city, Paul said: "Now there are varieties of gifts, but the same Spirit; and there are varieties of service, but the same Lord; and there are varieties of working, but it is the same God who inspires them all in every one. To each is given the manifestation of the Spirit for the common good" (1 Cor. 12:4-7). The emphasis of each of these is that of unique gifts or ministries or callings—all among the *laity*. Also in 1 Corinthians 12 Paul deals with the concept of the church as the "body of Christ." That is, each part has its own function and that function is *God-assigned.* The "ear" cannot be an "eye." There is nothing wrong with being an "eye," but the function of the "ear" is to *hear,* not to see! It is as though Paul is saying that the church is a "Spirit-gathered collection of gifts," each being brought to the Body for an express purpose. Each member has his function, his *assigned* function.

In the letter to the Church at Ephesus, a similar emphasis is made, but with unmistakable clarity. In chapter 4, he calls upon them (the people, not the pastor) to walk "worthy of their calling" (v. 1). He says: "But grace was given to each of us according to the measure of Christ's gift. Therefore it is said, 'When he ascended on high he led a host of captives, and he gave gifts to men' " (4:7-8). Each has his or her own calling; a gift or a ministry. And, the *pastor's* ministry is to "equip" them to exercise those gifts (vs. 11-12). Thus, we cannot say that so and so is called to the ministry with the idea that others are not called: *All Christians are called to the ministry.* The only question is *which ministry?* Some are called to be "equipping ministers" (the pastor); others are called to be teachers, singers, helpers, administrators, ad infinitum. Some of these gifts are to be exercised *inside* the church, as teaching; some are to be *outside* the church, as working with alcoholics or drug addicts or whatever.

Christ never intended the church to be like a bee hive with a queen bee, workers and drones! He intended it to be like a body with functioning parts and every part functioning!

This means, then, that not any "good work" will suffice! Only fulfilling your "calling" will suffice. It means that teaching a Sunday School class or being an usher or ministering at a state hospital may be wrong *for you!* Each of us has a specific assignment; we are endowed with a specific gift (or gifts); we are called to do something specific; to a particular ministry. Anything else, no matter how "good," puts us out of the will of God!

This, in turn, puts a burden of responsibility upon each of us to sort out our own gifts. We must find the Spirit of God within us and hear him out. And that is the "deeper life!" Many times, however, we shift this personal responsibility for discovering our own gifts to the nominating committee. We say, "You tell me what to do" and sidestep a responsibility which is uniquely ours. The nominating committee can very often be an instrument of the Spirit in helping us to discover our gifts and callings; but it can also be the evasion of it.

The recovery of *effective* Christianity rests in the rediscovery of the New Testament doctrine of the "ministry" being all-inclusive!

That was it! We had been thinking in terms of *groups* rather than *gifts;* of *good things* to do rather than *Christ's things* for us to do. We were going at it exactly backwards: starting groups to minister rather than finding ministries and grouping together those who had the same ministries. Indeed, some of those ministries might not even be a group function, they might be solely personal!

Out of this *breakthrough* of discovery came another discovery, a personal one for me. That is, I came to see that it was not my function to "think up" *good things* for Yokefellows or the church members to do! Rather, it is my function as a pastor, an "equipping minister," to help them *discover* their own ministries and then to *equip* them to fulfill *their* ministries.

Yet another spin-off of this discovery had to do with a new concept of the local church. If it is true that each has his own ministry and if it is true that the pastor exists to help the people discover and exercise their gifts, then, the church, in turn, must *provide channels* of ministry for the people. It is the concept that the church exists to support the people; the people do not exist solely to support the church! The church is to be the ally of the people, helping them to exercise what Christ has called them to do. This has tremendous and significant implications for the church that we, at Heritage are only beginning to grasp.

CHURCH PROGRAMMING

PARENTHETICALLY SPEAKING, imagine for a moment the significance for a church of the idea that every member has a ministry and that the church exists to discover, equip and provide a channel for it. Our present policy in local churches is relatively uniform. That is, the church staff "thinks up" good programs (and they are "good") and then the nominating committee attempts to enlist workers and participants. What if, however, a member comes and says that Christ has called him to minister to "drug addicts"? The typical response is: "We don't have a ministry to drug addicts; how about taking the junior high boys Sunday School class?"

There is nothing wrong with "taking the junior high boys Sunday School class"—if it is that person's *ministry*. But, what if Christ really did call him to minister to drug addicts?? Logically and biblically, that church should respond by training, equipping, and providing a channel for him to minister to drug addicts!

Taking the "ministry" idea seriously will mean some structural changes will be required, especially in terms of the training programs becoming more personalized, localized, and individualized. The only hindrance to a church making this transition is *vested interest in the traditional* as opposed to *vital interest in the tasks* assigned to its members by Christ!

Yet, in spite of the disappointment we were experiencing in our group venture, there was growth going on in the personal lives of the Yokefellows. The most obvious area of growth was love—the *agape* kind, the kind that kept them bound to each other even when our ideas were wrong. All of our meetings emphasize fellowship and love: *koinonia* and *agape*. We stress, over and over again, the necessity of both; they are the basic elements of renewal as water is the basic element for fish. Looking back upon it, I am more and more convinced that *koinonia* (fellowship) must precede *diakonia* (service); indeed, *koinonia* is the "atmosphere" which allows ministries and gifts to emerge.

Another area of growth was that of the *stewardship of possessions*. Not much was ever said about "tithing" or "giving to the church" in the Yokefellow meetings. The nature of the meetings precluded it. But, much was said about "giving" and "sharing" as the validation of our Christian experience. One by one, the couples came to see me privately! Most of them were young couples, just getting started, with small children and big debts, but they had come to see the necessity of biblical giving. How were they to start? I had some difficulty identifying with them, frankly, in that Aileen and I have always tithed. And, I had always preached that one should simply "start." In my own growth, however, I was coming to see through the eyes of others and of Christ. The suggestion which resulted was to begin *somewhere* and, by it, give expression to their liberation from *greed*—one of the basic offshoots of the self-centered life. Begin somewhere, at 2 percent or 5 percent and increase it until the tithe, the *minimum*, was reached. And, they did!

Growth was also obvious in many other ways. Several in the group made tremendous strides in emotional and marital growth. Still others literally "bloomed" into lovable and loving persons. A major cause of it was *personal devotions*. They were in the Word and in prayer on a regular basis, individually and as couples. They were also reading on their own, beyond the monthly studies, and they were growing from it. I was delightfully amazed at various times when they shared what they were reading and we began to regularly suggest good books to each other in the group. They were discovering Wallace Fisher, Elizabeth O'Connor, Deitrich Bonhoeffer, Findley Edge, and others. A number of them were subscribing to *Christianity Today* and *Faith-at-Work Magazine*. All of it not only deepened their lives, but also widened their perspective. And, although the small group venture was a disappointing disaster, they stayed and they grew! To learn how to fail successfully is a significant achievement in twentieth-century Christianity when all the roads are uncharted!

A MINIMUM DISCIPLINE

PARENTHETICALLY SPEAKING, a cursory investigation of these areas of growth (group involvement, stewardship, devotions, reading) will indicate that they represent the "minimum discipline" accepted by the group!

The Yokefellow "minimum discipline" requires: (1) daily Scripture and prayer; (2) weekly worship; (3) systematic giving; (4) Christ-filled vocations; (5) Christian reading; (6) unapologetic witnessing; and (7) group involvement. Keeping the "discipline" before the group paid-off *silently!* One simply cannot do it without spiritual benefit!

We strongly suggest to any group the adoption of a "minimum discipline" whether it be the Yokefellow one or one put together by the group themselves. We do not require a "pledge" to do it of any member; we do say, however, that a *Yokefellow* is one who. . . . One can "attend" Yokefellows without being a Yokefellow and no one is asked to "report" on their activities along this line. One "becomes" a Yokefellow on his own.

Finally, there was one other area of Yokefellow growth. It was during this period that a number of the group moved away from Annapolis. One was transferred by his company to Indiana, another to California. Three professors at the Academy, who were in the group, finished their enlistment and left: one to a job in California, one to graduate school in Michigan, and the other to further Navy service in Rhode Island. The growth? "Yokefellow-like" groups began to emerge in Indiana, California, Michigan, and Rhode Island! We have since come to see this as a part of our "stewardship" of renewal and, now, one can only leave as a "missionary"!

This was especially true of one particular Yokefellow couple. He had moved to Annapolis with his work as a technical writer for a major electronics firm. But, he became tired of "running" when he arrived. Early in his life, he had accepted Christ into his life and came to see that Christ's ministry for him was preaching the gospel. But, he ran . . . successfully . . . for a while . . . until it caught up with him. He sought a compensation for it by becoming a lay minister in the Scientology movement, finally leaving his job to do it full-time. But, it too proved empty. He once again entered the field of technical writing and that was when he came to Annapolis. Seventeen years of running, from age seventeen to age thirty-four, had taken its toll, however, and he began to pray himself toward surrender. But, it was hard . . . *really hard:* his income was substantial now and, besides, his wife was an atheist who had never been to a church! One morning, he broke. He yielded. Expression was given to it by the writing of a biographical letter of the whole prodigal venture up to and including his decision. But, he did not know to whom to send it. He did not know a pastor!

Now, you are not going to believe this—if you don't believe that the Spirit of God is at work in the world—but he did two things. First, he picked my name out of the "Yellow Pages" and sent the letter to me. Second, he prayed to meet someone who could guide him. That day, he met a neighbor couple who invited them to church! Not just any church, however, but to Heritage Church! They were *Yokefellows!*

The extended outgrowth of it was the reaffirmation of his call, the baptism of his wife, his enrollment in Southern Baptist Theological Seminary in Louisville, and his call to be the pastor of a church in Indiana! At their last meeting with us, we had prayer together. I prefaced it with a talk about Paul and Barnabas being "sent away" on their first missionary tour (Acts 13) and of how they "laid hands" on them in a symbolic endorsement of their ministries. God had called them; this was *their* ministry, and the laying on of hands was the church's concurrence in it. But, as in Antioch, so in Annapolis, it was not only a sign of their *endorsement of,* but also of their *involvement in* those ministries. Consequently, as we bowed together, I asked any present who felt led to do so, to lay hands on them in the spirit of endorsement and involvement. One by one, they did. It was a "moving" time of commitment for all of us. This is the only time we have ever done this, but it serves to point out that Yokefellows are responsible for what they know—wherever they go!

6. COME ON IN, THE WATER'S FINE

We would see Jesus, also! (John 12:21, author's interpretation).

The Manresa Retreat had a *reverberating* effect upon the people at Heritage, as well as upon the Yokefellow group. The most immediate effect was the churchwide realization that the Yokefellow movement in the church was doing "something" in the lives of those involved. When the group members came forward during the invitation period the Sunday morning following the retreat to express their commitments to me, it "shook" the church family. They had seen the group grow in number; now they were seeing the group grow in spirit. In one climactic moment, "Yokefellows" became a "part" of Heritage!

But, *serendipity!* There was more. A group of our median age adults approached me later in the week. Like the Greeks who came to the disciples wanting to "see Jesus, too," these adults said, "We would like to have a Yokefellow group for our age group, too!" I had not thought in terms of "another Yokefellow group"; my idea had been merely to continue to enlarge the existing group. Experience had already evidenced that the age groups have their own peculiar sets of relational needs and this request was evidently of the Spirit: a second "cluster" of groups, operating just like the Yokefellow group—Yoke groups! It fell into place as though Someone had just "handed" us the piece of the puzzle which had been missing. What else could be done? Yokefellow *Two* was born!

Summer is devastating to the church program in Annapolis. So many of our people work in the academic world with summers off, plus the large group of government workers who enjoy rather liberal vacation periods, plus the fact that most people live in Annapolis because of the Chesapeake Bay and boating (with only weekends available for using them), that our church program all out grinds to a halt. The group approached me in May and, because of the season, we decided to put it off until fall.

In September, 1971, a public announcement was issued that a "Yokefellow Two" group was being considered. For those who were interested, a time and a place was established to meet and discuss the possibilities.

There were a half dozen couples from the forty-to-sixty age group who came. At the meeting, I shared with them what and how the Yokefellow One (their new name!) functioned. The Yokefellow Two group, I said, need not and should not be a duplicate version of Yokefellow One. However, I stressed that the *objectives* should be clearly understood: that the group existed to *encourage* and *enable* the members to find a *deeper* and a *wider* spiritual life by meeting together for *study* along the lines of the *practical* (rather than the theoretical) and the *positive* (rather than the negative).

GROUP EMPHASES

PARENTHETICALLY SPEAKING, we are more and more *convinced* of the validity of these twin emphases in renewal groups: be *practical* and be *positive.* So many times, church people define a "good meeting" as being a "good argument." We meet and we argue, mostly on some theoretical issue which will not make any difference in any one's life or relationships. Each states his opinions, half-hears the others, and leaves. No one is changed, helped, encouraged, or strengthened!

Thus, we *stress* in Yokefellows that we meet *only* for the "practical." We deal with *life,* our *Christian* lives—on the basis of "How?" Likewise, we stress the "positive" as opposed to "negative criticism." Anyone can say what is wrong—and it is easy to find something wrong. But, that offers little help to strugglers. What is *right* and how to get on with it—those are *the* questions. Hence, at times, we have to exercise *self-restraint* and, at times, *group discipline.* We have to "lay down and play dead" with some questions—if it is merely a theoretical, vacuum-tube truth or a negative remark without the person saying "we" (instead of "they") and paralleling it with the positive. Consequently, in six years-plus, there has never been an "argument" about an abstract issue!

The idea of the "minimum discipline" was also introduced, again stressing that no one can "join" Yokefellows. There is nothing to join! One can only "become" a Yokefellow by accepting the discipline and doing it, no questions asked.

After talking it over for nearly an hour, this group decided to proceed. They agreed to meet once per month (later settling on the third Friday of each month), using the same format as Yokefellow One (studying a book together), and to emphasize the "minimum discipline." One of the couples in the group offered their home for the meeting place.

The first meeting of "Yokefellow Two" was in October, 1971. We discussed various beginning points and emphases, and decided to begin with the study of Bruce Larson's *Dare to Live Now.* A chapter was taken at each monthly meeting with a brief summary being given and discussion following. Other books which followed it were *The Taste of New Wine*, Keith Miller; *Extraordinary Living for Ordinary Man*, Samuel Shoemaker; and *Setting Men Free*, Bruce Larson.

Yokefellow Two benefited from the experience of Yokefellow One in many ways. This was especially true with regard to the necessity of *koinonia* (fellowship) being prerequisite to *diakonia* (ministry). Consequently, from the very beginning it emphasized communal fellowship. This process was aided by incorporating relational activities and buzz groups to the discussion period. At one of the early meetings, the "Quaker Questions" were used. (Where did you live between the ages of seven and twelve, and how many brothers and sisters were at home? How did you heat your house? Who was the warmest person in your life? When did God become more than a word to you?) In another, questions like, "In what room of the house are you most 'you'?" and "What do you like best about God?" were asked. Questions like these allow us to "open up" and to know and be known, thereby hastening *koinonia*. On another occasion, a discussion on the home was supplemented by each member bending a pipe cleaner into a symbolic representation of "the perfect family" and explaining it. In perhaps less than half the time required for Yokefellow One, Yokefellow Two made the transition from *ekklesia* (the assembly) to the *koinonia* (the fellowship)!

As with Yokefellow One, great emphasis was also given to the *practical* and the *positive* in all of our study and discussion. This is, however, far easier to say than to do! We are so conditioned to the *theoretical* and the *negative* in the Christian movement that it is difficult to "lay down and play dead" with some questions and issues. Yet with repetition and reinforcement it can come.

After the study of four books, Yokefellow Two made yet another change from the style of Yokefellow One. As we neared the end of the book, as always, I raised the question of the next one. What are our felt needs? Witnessing? Discipline? And, I suggested some books. Someone raised the idea of a "Bible study" of some sort. They liked it. I did not. From the very beginning of our Yokefellow involvement at Heritage, I felt that the monthly meetings should be for book studies rather than Bible study. This is not to say that the Bible was not studied. Rather, it was a question of starting with a book and going to the Bible for illustrative matter rather than the reverse. I felt that this was the better way if we were trying to reach "outsiders." To be invited to "study the Bible" in a meeting "led by our pastor" sounded too much like "church" to me! Yet, I had determined from the outset of our work to let the groups exist *for the people*, at *their* points of need. So, I agreed.

At the meeting, however, I laid some ground rules! I explained my reluctance to do it, but that I existed to equip *them*. Knowing the group as I did, and loving each other as we did, I was able to say that I "knew" some of them well enough to know that they liked to "argue the Bible." Our emphasis must be *practical* and must relate to the living of the Christ-life, I said. They acknowledged the truth of it and "contracted" to stay away from the theoretical issues which would not make any difference in our daily lives. (Thus, the origin of "Cain's wife" and other similar questions were "solved" in advance!) My study suggestions were Ephesians; Colossians; John; a study of the Holy Spirit; or perhaps the seven churches of Revelation. They chose the latter. We started at the next meeting after I suggested a couple of books to study in advance: William Barclay's *The Revelation of John* and/or Charles Erdman's *The Revelation of John.*

But, the study was different than they expected! A difference they came to appreciate and which made a difference in how they studied the Bible afterwards on a personal basis! I prefaced the study by reviewing the various interpretations of Revelation, particularly that, to some, the seven churches mentioned in Revelation represented successive "ages" through which Christianity must pass before the second coming. However, the Yokefellow Two would treat the seven letters to these churches as letters to *actual, living congregations,* looking for practical truths relevant to a group of Christians just like us.

To accomplish this, I prefaced each monthly study with a ten-minute overview of the interpretation problems of each letter, and, henceforth, we finished with them! Then, I would pass our mimeographed sheets with questions on them for the group members to answer. We would do this by breaking up into small "buzz groups" of five or six, dealing with the assigned questions, and reporting back after an hour of group study. Having "assigned questions" solved two problems: (1) staying away from the theoretical problems which could "bog" us down and (2) insuring that I could convey a practical approach to Bible study which they could apply both in their daily lives and in their personal Bible reading. This latter emphasis, equipping them to read the Bible, was the primary motive. This, then, became our format—a format still being used by Yokefellow Two at this writing and a feature which further distinguishes them from Yokefellow One. (Several of these studies are in Appendix E.) Presently, the group is studying the Ten Commandments, using Elton Trueblood's *Foundations for Reconstruction.*

During this period, the group sifted and settled in "membership"—for want of a better term since there is nothing to join. Attendance varied from ten or twelve at the beginning to twenty-five or thirty. After a year or so, it settled down to a core group of twenty, mostly couples in the middle age bracket of forty to sixty. The majority are members of Heritage along with a Catholic and several "Protestants."

The group meets in one of two homes, both with large living rooms to accommodate the group. This is another variation from Yokefellow One which meets in the same place each month.

MEETING LOCATION

PARENTHETICALLY SPEAKING, we strongly suggest that the larger monthly meeting meet regularly in one place for several reasons. One is that it solves the communication problem of "where are we meeting this month?" Then, too, some would want the group, but their accommodations might not be the best. It requires a large room where people can sit in a circle with no "back rows." Also, some might feel reluctant to become involved if they thought they were "obligated" to host the group in return.

Yokefellow One meets in one place; Yokefellow Two in no more than two. The small groups, however, do hold their meetings in various homes. With them, though, the number of those attending is such as to solve the space and notification problems.

Across the period between October, 1971, and February, 1973, Yokefellow Two grew; growing where it counts, that is. They grew "upward" in their spiritual lives and they grew "together" in the mesh of the Spirit. They were ready for their "Manresa" and the move toward small groups. A retreat was suggested and it found ready, if not eager, acceptance. It was scheduled for February 17, 1973, at the Manresa Retreat Center with the theme: "Toward Koinonia."

YOKEFELLOW TWO RETREAT

Manresa Retreat House   February 17, 1973   Annapolis, Maryland

"Toward Koinonia"

9:00	Koffee and Koinonia
9:15	Bible Study on Koinonia

9:45	Break
10:00	Study of *Groups Alive-Church Alive*
10:50	Break
11:00	Study of *Groups Alive-Church Alive*
12:00	Free Time
12:30	Lunch
1:30	Important Things About Groups
2:00	Break
2:15	Book Reports on Koinonia by Yokefellows
	Farewell to the Lonely Crowd
	Visualization Prayer
	No Longer Strangers
3:00	Break
3:15	Small Group Activity
4:00	Break
4:15	Music and Thoughts on Koinonia
4:45	Time Alone
5:15	Free for Fellowship
6:00	Dinner
7:00	Share-and-Prayer Time

The morning was spent in a study of small group dynamics. As Yokefellow Two was obviously tending in that direction, they needed to be aware of it as was true with Yokefellow One. This time, however, rather than teach it myself as before, I exercised my "equipping ministry" by asking a member of Yokefellow One to do it! He had sat through the course before and I had noticed an evident interest in it by him. I took that as a "clue" and asked him to do it this time. (It is now one of his *ministries* as he does it at all of our retreats and has also shared it with other churches and conferences.)

The afternoon and evening were given to an exploration of *koinonia* via small groups. We looked at our theme of "Toward Koinonia" by discussing reports from the members of the group on various books. We used *Groups Alive-Church Alive* as the basic study, supplementing it with reports from John Drakeford's *Farewell to the Lonely Crowd* and Bruce Larson's *No Longer Strangers*.

Since our retreats are "decisional retreats," the late afternoon was given over to *decisions* (rather than *conclusions*) about *koinonia*. A tape recorder provided a musical background to "thoughts" about *koinonia* flashed on the overhead projector screen. The "thought" was kept before us for a minute or so, and then another "thought."

After this quiet time, each retreatant was asked to spend some time alone or in an "Emmaus Walk"—coming to a commitment concerning *koinonia* in *their* lives and in *our* group.

The evening was spent in sharing and prayer together as we sought the mind of Christ *for us*. It was a "Manresa time" for them, too, as had been true of Yokefellow One's first retreat. But, it was not the same. That is, Yokefellow One's BREAKTHROUGH had been an enthusiastic, almost overwhelming "experience." Not so with Yokefellow Two! The *impact* was equally as powerful, but their *response* was "quiet acceptance." One element of their "acceptance" was small groups: they decided to move in a direction similar to Yokefellow One—the monthly meeting with small groups issuing from it as spokes from a hub. While no specific groups or ministries were expressed, within a month a Bible study group started. It meets once per month, led by a Yokefellow Two-er who has an undeniable gift of teaching. It immediately reached a whole segment of our church family that I had been totally unable to reach through Yokefellows or the church program! The "idea" of renewal is more important than who conveys it and, by equipping another, it was done!

The other element of their "acceptance" had to do with a definition of *koinonia* and a decision to accept that definition for Yokefellow Two—as both a group and an individual covenant. No one remembers the source of the definition, who suggested it or even when it emerged during the day. (Which probably says something about its true Source!) It has since been shared with Yokefellow One and other groups with great acceptance. But, it is more than just a definition; the key was their *acceptance of* it and their common *obedience to* it. It shaped a group of people into a *fellowship*. There is no *explanation* of Yokefellow Two apart from it! We said . . . and *accepted:* "Koinonia" is being as committed to each other as we are to Christ. Think about it.

7. AND THEY CAME BEARING GIFTS

Having gifts that differ according to the grace given to us, let us use them (Rom. 12:6).

As Yokefellow One came to the point of redirection, it was evident that the problem had been that of thinking in terms of *groups* rather than *gifts*. As the small groups which grew out of the Manresa Retreat experience began either to fail or flounder, it caused some deep introspection among the group members. The extended outgrowth of it was a second retreat, a "rethinking" retreat. (See chapter 5.) This time, instead of "groups," our theme was "gifts."

The date was Saturday, October 7, 1972. It was now seventeen months since the Manresa Retreat of May, 1971. The planning of the retreat was as before with the Yokefellows themselves doing both the planning and leading. The retreat, "Our Quest for Our Gifts," took place at Pine Lane Retreat Center just outside Annapolis.

YOKEFELLOW ONE RETREAT

Pine Lane   October 7, 1972   Annapolis, Maryland

"OUR QUEST ... FOR ... OUR GIFTS"
There's a Sweet Spirit in this Place

9:00-9:50 .... Coffee and Questions
9:50-10:00 .... A Break!

10:00-10:45	The Deeper Life: Pastor
10:45-11:00	Another Break!
11:00-12:00	Study of Group Dynamics
12:00-12:30	Free Time—Talk a Walk!
12:30-1:30	Lunch
1:30-2:30	Book Presentations: Yokefellows

        1:30-1:50 *Eighth Day of Creation*
        1:50-2:10 *Touch of the Spirit*
        2:10-2:20 *You Are a Potter*
        2:20-2:30 *Greening of the Church*

2:30-2:40	Yet Another Break!
2:40-3:40	Your Neighbor's Gifts: The Group
3:40-3:50	And One More Break!
3:50-4:20*	Group Quiet! Gifts Being Born: The Group
4:20-5:00	Quiet Time—Alone and Away
5:00-6:00	Free Time
6:00-7:00	Dinner
7:00-8:00	Sharing Time: The Group
8:00-9:00	Celebration: In the Chapel

 The morning hours were spent in a "restudy" of (1) the deeper life and (2) group dynamics. We felt that the group needed it as a refresher course and that the newer members needed it for orientation purposes. I led the study on the deeper life as my contribution to the retreat.[1] My original intention had been to also lead the dynamics review. But, on a "holy hunch," I asked one of the Yokefellows to do it, one who had been through the course at the Manresa Retreat. I was right "on target." He accepted it and was later to do it at the Yokefellow Two retreat (see previous chapter) and at each subsequent retreat.

 During the afternoon, we "got down to business" with the theme of *gifts*. Three group members shared ideas gleaned from various books on the subject: *The Touch of the Spirit* by Ralph Neighbour, which was our common study book for the retreat; *The Eighth Day of Creation* by Elizabeth O'Connor; and *The Greening of the Church* by Findley Edge.

 After a break, the group regathered to spend some time "sorting out" the gifts of others. That is, we called to each other's attention those gifts which we could see in each other. By this, we felt that gifts might be called forth or confirmed by others. It was stressed that this was not to be confused with good "characteristics" or "personality traits" in others. Rather, we were looking for *gifts*—ministries which we felt the others might be able to do. Ralph Neighbour mentions in his *The Touch of the Spirit* that many of us have our ministries "built in" to us already: some talent or ability which can be an *entreé* for a ministry. (For instance, one suggestion was that a physical education instructor in our group might be able to develop a "slimnastics" program for women, using it as a medium to share about *inner* strength and beauty, too.)

Then from 4:00 to 5:00 P.M., we came to a new element of our retreat practices: *time alone*. On the program it was labeled: "Group Quiet—Gifts Being Born!" The first half hour was spent together. Tape recorded music provided a contemplative background as "thoughts" were flashed, one by one, on the screen from the overhead projector, as was done at the previously mentioned Yokefellow Two retreat. There were such thoughts as:

"I was afraid and went out and hid my talent" (see Matt. 25:25).

"Creativeness in the world is, as it were, the eighth day of creation" (Berdyaev).

If you have nothing to create, create yourself.

"I appeal to you, brethren, present your bodies a living sacrifice to God" (see Rom. 12:1).

Why did God make you a "gift" to us?

"Having gifts that differ . . . let us use them" (Rom. 12:6).

The second half-hour segment was spent alone as group members ventured out onto the grounds by themselves. The specific intention behind this "time alone" was the assessment of our gifts: what is God "calling" *me* to do? What is *my* "ministry"?

TIMES ALONE

PARENTHETICALLY SPEAKING, the idea of a "time alone" has become an integral part of our Heritage retreat procedure. It is a definite time of the program where the retreatants are requested to get away—and alone—with God and themselves. (Sometimes this is adapted as an "Emmaus Walk" where two retreatants go together in quest of the mysterious Third One to company with them.)

However, this is more than a "coffee break" or a designated

"fellowship" period. Those are a part of the program, too. But, this "time alone" is for *introspection, communion, assessment,* and, above all, *commitment.* Sometimes this has to do with the theme of the particular retreat; at least, that is our intention. We have found, however, that many times it focuses on other things. Like a sin with which we must deal *before* any significant commitments can be made!

The all but unaminous report of the Yokefellows is that the "time alone" is always the *most productive part* of every retreat. This is probably the case because it provides an occasion for those "teachable moments" so necessary to Christian growth, times of quiet waiting before the Lord when we let him "have *his* say."

The day was climaxed after dinner as the group gathered in the chapel to share their "reports." Sitting in Quaker fashion, with everyone facing toward the center of the room, each spoke as they chose to do so. After a time of awkward silence, one stood, walked to center and "reported" to the rest of us that God had "made clear" a ministry to her. Then, another came. And another. And another! Until all of the group of twenty-five or so had "reported in." Some reported *obvious* ministries; others reported *possible* ministries; still others reported *no* ministries. But, each "reported in" and each asked for the prayers of the group. Totally different from the "climax" of the Manresa Retreat, this one was deeply serious. The mood was one of the acceptance of responsibility, like that of an elder son at the death of a father.

As the members each "reported in," some "conclusions" became progressively obvious. Without any "comparison of notes," they seemed to be saying the things over and over again.

ABOUT GIFTS

PARENTHETICALLY SPEAKING, we discovered such startling things as these:

1. *That Christ does give "gifts" to people!* These gifts are more than talents and abilities, however. They are ministries and functions by which we *serve* others. As is always true, "gifts" are for others: a gift is something we give to another. God's gifts to us are, in a sense, not gifts *to* us but *for* us—to

give to others. When our children were smaller, before "allowances" or "paper routes," Aileen and I did as most parents do at Christmas. That is, I would take Karen or Steven or Philip "Christmas shopping" and buy gifts for them to give to Aileen. She did the same with them for me. *We were giving gifts to them to give to another.* That is the way of Christ's "gifts" to us. They are gifts to be given, not gifts to be received!

2. *That Christ makes gifts of people!* Not only does he make gifts "to" people, he also makes gifts "of" people. When Paul speaks of Christ's gifts to the assembly, as reported in Ephesians 4:1-16, the gifts mentioned are *persons!* He "gave" us apostles, prophets, evangelists, pastors, etc.—*persons*. In other words, he did not give us "the position of apostle"; he gave us "apostles"! The reports of the group confirmed and reconfirmed that each of us was a gift *to the group* and to various individual members of the group. This, in a sense, stresses the "Body" concept of 1 Corinthians 12, that the Spirit brings the various parts of the Body together to make a functioning *whole* as each part complements the others.

3. *That not all ministries are "group" ministries.* Our first attempt had been to start groups centered around various needs or tasks. But, we had confused "doing good things" with "exercising our gifts." *Good* things are not always the same as *Christ's* things! For instance, when Paul set out on his second missionary tour, it was his intention to take the gospel into new areas of Asia Minor. After visiting several of the churches initiated on the first tour, he arrived in the region of Galatia—the farthest point of his first journey. From there Paul intended to go westward into the province of Asia, the tiny province from which the whole continent got its name. But, they "were forbidden of the Holy Spirit to preach the word in Asia" (Acts 16:6)! Next, they decided to take the gospel northward to the province of Bithynia, but "the Spirit did not allow them" (16:7)! Coming, then, to Troas, the Spirit led them to where he intended: to Europe! Now, there was nothing wrong with taking the gospel to Asia or Bithynia. It was a "good" thing; but it was not "Christ's" thing *for them* to do!

Yokefellow One came to see this important distinction. Having grasped that, we were then able to see that our first quest should be *gifts* not *groups.* The "gift" *precedes* the "group" and, in some instances, *precludes* a group. That is, a gift may not be a "group ministry." For instance, one might see his gift as a ministry to alcoholics. Others might sense that as their ministry, too, and a group is formed. Another, however, may see his gift as teaching which does not require a group of teachers. Some ministries, then, are "personal" ministries. We are convinced that the "group" is the best method for the discovery of one's gifts, groups like the Yokefellow group, but that gifts do not always function through a group. Some do; others do not.

But, "conclusions" are not the sole objective of a retreat. One could conceivably come to these "conclusions" and still never exercise his or her gifts! Thus, retreats must also be "decisional." All of our retreats have that common goal: commitment. (One Yokefellow recently chose not to attend a retreat for this very reason. He shared with the group that business pressures had made such a havoc of his spiritual life that he was not ready to "make any commitments." While the group disagreed, they accepted it; but the emphasis here is that he knew of the *decisional* nature of the retreat.) And, such was the case with this retreat.

Another phrase was added to the Yokefellow One vocabulary: *"after Pine Lane"!* It, too, was a *pivotal point* in many of our lives, just as was "Manresa." It is not uncommon to hear Yokefellows say, "Before Manresa" or "After Pine Lane" because both of these retreats were pivotal experiences. The names, "Manresa" and "Pine Lane," are insignificant in themselves, however indebted we are for those responsible for providing such places for retreats. This was, no doubt, also true of our New Testament counterparts. I am sure that they said such things as "before Pentecost" or "after Damascus Road" or "since the Macedonian vision." The important things were not the Jewish holiday, nor the location of Damascus, nor the geography of Macedonia. Rather, the important things were *the encounters with their destinies and their decisions!* These, too, were pivotal points. More and more, I am convinced that the normal

Christian life is lived out in a series of "peaks" and "plateaus"; the kind of life which can be "plotted" on a graph with a series of dots representing crisis turning points. For Yokefellows, those "dots" are invariably our retreats and this is the case because we have made them *decisional* retreats.

At Pine Lane, some of those "decisions" were made. Others committed themselves to decide when their gifts became clear. In the weeks and months which followed Pine Lane, "gifts" began to emerge! Some emerged into groups; others emerged as personal ministries. Some were known *before* Pine Lane; some *at* Pine Lane; some *after* it. But, "Pine Lane" was the "dot" on the graph. It was the point and place of a BREAKTHROUGH! Each "gift" was reported to the whole group; a few at Pine Lane, but most came in the monthly Yokefellow meetings which followed it. For instance: one of our Yokefellows worked as a secretary at a State Hospital and had been taking courses in "Family Therapy" to further her vocation. She came to see this as a "ministry." We now have a family therapy program at the church!

Another Yokefellow stated at Pine Lane that her "ministry" had to do with "flower arranging," a thing she enjoyed and something she sensed as a "touch point" with the world for ministry. (Several of us frankly raised eyebrows at the strangeness of this statement.) After several months, she began making flower arrangements to take to lonely people at a nearby nursing home, providing an occasion for conversation and witness!

Yet another saw his ministry as "encouragement." Having known him, as we did, we knew that if it was his "gift" it would have to be a "gift"—he did not have it among his basic personality equipment! Today, all of us have been "kept on our feet" at one or another by his gift. The miraculous element in it, which indicates it is not an affected habit, is that he also knows when it is needed!

Unbeknownst to us, one Yokefellow had been fighting becoming involved with the group of ladies ministering at the State Hospital. As a student nurse, she had done some of her training in such a place and it has proved too much of an emotional drain on her. She "yielded" to it, however, and is now the unspoken leader of the group!

One young couple was "open to whatever," as they said it at Pine Lane. We had previously started a group for career-singles which had floundered. On a "holy hunch" I approached them about leading it. It was not a "nominating committee" approach, however, trying to talk them into it. Rather, I saw in them the qualities necesary for it and called it to their attention. Several weeks later they assumed it and it is now one of our most effective ministries!

One Yokefellow saw no gifts, but she did have a desire to "pray." In a series of attempts and steps, she came to see her ministry as "intercessory prayer." She now is "available" every Friday morning from 10:00 A.M. until noon for others to stop by and pray with her in her home or to call and ask for her prayers!

Another young man who had been an eagle scout as a boy, saw clearly that his scouting experience was a built-in touch point with boys. He became our assistant scoutmaster and has infused the troop with a dynamic witness!

A couple, both librarians, saw their ministry in books. But, how? The result: they now operate a "book table" in the church, offering Christian books for sale to our members on Sunday mornings. Done on a nonprofit basis, they secure the books from a local Christian book store on consignment each week. And, the Word is spread!

And, on and on the list grew from October 7, 1972—"after Pine Lane." And, the BREAKTHROUGH? It was . . . *Gifts First, Not Groups!*

Notes

1. See the author's *Renew My Church*, Chapter 9.

8. DEEP AND WIDE, DEEP AND WIDE

And he appointed twelve, to be with him, and to be sent out (Mark 3:14).

The seven months which followed the Pine Lane retreat on "gifts" was a compounded miracle of ministry. It was as though every seed planted over the previous five years came to fruition. Gifts and ministries emerged among the group members and seemed to spark other gifts and ministries into being in the process.

These new ministries and groups brought about an "engagement" with the world. After Manresa, that "engagement" also came. But, when it came to the point of "evangelism-engagement," they backed off. Now, however, the group members seemed willing and able to "mix it" with the world, bearing witness and sharing their own "interim reports" of Christ's activity in their lives.

Then, it happened again. They began to back off.

This time, it was not at the point of *engagement*, but at the point of *effectiveness*. Somehow, they thought that every "witness-given" would be a "convert-gained!" But, it did not work that way. There were a few miracle stories, but even they seemed to discourage rather than encourage the group. They asked, "Why doesn't this happen when *I* witness?" One couple was out for a walk one evening, after praying every day for opportunities to witness, and met another couple—and won them. They joined the church! Another Yokefellow met a young man in the apartment complex where they both lived and, through friendship, was able to help him over a spiritual hurdle and into the church—and eventually into the pastoral ministry! But, this was not the case with others. The "Ladies Day Out" group were able to get their unchurched friends involved, but could not win them. The group working at the state hospital had previously only "helped out" in the ward. After Pine Lane, they sought to also witness. But, getting the gospel through the emotional and physchological maze proved all but impossible. Various men in the group began to "own up" to their Christian commitment at work, but with no observable results. In my role as pastor, I encountered several new couples and "assigned" Yokefellow couples to befriend them in hopes of winning them. They did not.

Month after month, the Yokefellows returned to the monthly meeting more and more discouraged. They were elated that they could witness and were amazed at the help the Holy Spirit had given them time and time again. But, the absence of results completely demoralized them.

In April, six months after Pine Lane, we met as usual for our monthly meeting. We began, as always, with the "reports" from the groups and the various ministries. It was lackluster at best. Then, as always, I asked if there was a "felt" need for a group or a new ministry or whatever. After a brief hesitation, someone spoke. And, it only "primed the pump." Others followed, one by one, and all on the same subject: *the ineffectiveness of their witness.* They discussed it, back and forth, looking for reasons. They readily agreed that it was somehow tied to their inner lives and the ministry of the Holy Spirit. But, how? And, then, someone suggested that it was "time for another retreat."

THE PACE OF RENEWAL

PARENTHETICALLY SPEAKING, this, too, is a part of the Heritage pattern: the suggestions coming from the people at the point of desparation. More and more, I am convinced that the normal Christian life is one of *crisis* "peaks" and "plateaus," and, for us, those peaks have been "retreats." Nonetheless, we do not preplan them. Rather, it has been my attempt to allow the need to grow among them until it is a groundswell and they *have* to have it. This, in itself, is almost positive assurance of success. An annual spring or fall retreat is not always so. When they are hungry, they will eat! When the growth pattern is adjusted *to their pace,* rather than programmed according to the "church calendar," it is far more effective. This does not mean that it cannot be mentioned as a "possibility," but rather that the *time of need* is the critical factor in renewal programming.

The suggestion of a retreat was quickly accepted. It seemed that once the need was out in the open, everyone confirmed it. The topic was no problem because it was the "point of need" for us. There was some difficulty in articulating it, however, because we had always had single-topic retreats before. This one apparently had two: *witnessing* and the *devotional* life. No matter how we approached it in our discussion, the two seemed tied together: the inner life of devotion and the outer life of witness.

An ad hoc committee of two couples was appointed by the group to plan the retreat. A place was secured (Manresa again) and the planning group met at our house. My contribution was to clarify how the two elements, the inner and outer lives, fit together, but the actual planning was theirs. Their choices were a surprise. Always before we had depended upon the shared experiences and expertise of the group members as resource people. But, the expressed feeling was that all the group could share on these topics were their frustrations and defeats. They asked for a "led" retreat. But, who? The result was a program to be led primarily by Aileen and the wife of the associate pastor, Wilma Wild, and me! To anyone familiar with the maturation cycle in the small group process, this has significant meaning. That is, there is a predictable pattern through which groups go in terms of leadership views: from dependence upon the expert to rejection (in prodigal son fashion) and, hopefully, to reacceptance of the leadership in the sense of accepting the leadership when it is needed. To me, this represented a step of greater significance than they were realized. I saw it as the fulfillment of *my gift*—as the "equipper" of the saints—and, more importantly, their affirmation of it.

The date was set for Saturday, May 12, 1973. There was no single book to be found on the twin topics of witnessing and the inner life. Thus, two books, both by Elton Trueblood, were suggested: *The New Man for Our Time* (chapters 1-4) and my *Renew My Church* (chapters 4-5).

YOKEFELLOW ONE RETREAT
Manresa Retreat House   May 12, 1973   Annapolis, Maryland
"INNER LIFE: DEVOTIONS
OUTER LIFE: WITNESSING"

9:00-9:30	Devotions for Today
9:30-10:15	Sharing Time: Devotional Questions
10:15-10:30	Break
10:30-11:15	Developing a Meaningful Inner Life
11:15-11:30	Break
11:30-11:50	My Life of Prayer
11:50-12:10	My Life of Devotional Reading
12:30-1:30	LUNCH
1:30-2:15	Personal Factors in Witnessing
2:15-2:30	Break
2:30-3:15	Witnessing: Personal & Group
3:15-3:30	Break
3:30-4:15	"Moving From The Inside Out"-Tape by Keith Miller
4:15-4:30	Break
4:30-	Sharing Time: Witnessing
6:00-7:00	DINNER
7:00-8:00	A Celebration of Commitment
8:00	Home!!

The morning hours were given over the *devotional life;* the afternoon to *witnessing.* Aileen and Wilma shared their own pattern on Bible reading (Aileen) and prayer (Wilma). This in itself, was an acknowledgment on the part of the group. Neither Aileen nor Wilma are actively involved in the Yokefellow activities except for the retreats. Wilma is involved with her husband in the youth activities of the church and Aileen in the education program for adults as the teacher of the theology course, plus the "expected" activities of both in the total church. Additionally, both have three children to which they must be mother and part-time fathers. But, the group (as others) recognized something in both of them which they attributed to their devotional lives: a calmness, a quiet confidence, an unhurried grasp on life. The group wanted to know "why?" and, more importantly, "how?" Thus, they were asked to share it.

Sorting through the experience-truths they shared, common elements were readily seen. (1) Both acknowledged that Bible reading and prayer can be *separated only in theory, not in practice.* They go together or not at all. One must pray, then read, then pray again. That is, one must preface Bible reading with a prayer for openness to God's truth; then, read with the eyes coupled to the spiritual ears to "hear" the Word; and, finally, commit the biblical truth through prayer into practice. Both acknowledged this three-step process. (2) Both also shared the necessity of a *definite time and place* for a devotional life. Being mothers, both reported that this revolved around their children—or rather, their absence! It had to be done when they were at school or asleep! But, both stressed that it had to be a disciplined experience. (3) Finally, Aileen and Wilma both acknowledged that there are *"places" to read in the Bible,* places where God is heard "more clearly" than others. God can speak to us through any passage of the Bible, they said, but some are "more audible." This was a real "clue" for all of us. For Aileen, these were the Psalms and the Gospels. For Wilma, the Epistles and Proverbs. For many in the group, this was a great insight: that there are "places to look." For instance, compare Matthew 1:1-16 with John 3:1-16. Any rabbit hunter knows that rabbits can appear most any place but also that there are places to look for them, too. Just as any mother knows that the children's dirty socks can appear any place in the house, but there are places to look (under the bed!) and places *not* to look (in the dirty clothes basket!). Experience teaches us that about the Bible, too.

Wilma illustrated this by ending the morning with a Bible reading for the group. She noted that the book of Proverbs has thirty-one chapters, as though it was planned for a month of reading! She chose chapter 12 since it was the date of the retreat. As she read it aloud, everyone of us found a verse in it, "tailor-made" for us, and each was different![1]

The afternoon was given to a study of *witnessing.* By a process of sharing our personal experiences, listening to a tape by Keith

Miller [2] and some teaching on my part,[3] several clues about our witnessing were gained.

First, witnessing is essentially *our personal reports* of Christ's activity in *our* own lives. That is, "witnessing," strictly speaking, is what one has seen and heard, personally. As a noun, to witness is to "personally observe something." As a verb, it is to "report" what has been observed. It is not passing out tracts, quoting Scripture verses or preaching a one-to-one sermon. It may *include* these things, but witnessing is not to be *identified* with any or all of them. One does not necessarily have to personally experience anything to pass out tracts or quote Scripture! In fact, a *pagan* can do that! But, witnessing *requires* experience; indeed, an *up-dated* experience!

Second, witnessing is done on an "as you go" basis. That is, witnessing is not something you "go and do"; it is something you "do as you go." It best occurs in the normal flow of daily activities. This was true of Jesus. The great experiences of witness by Christ occurred within the normal course of events: people came to him or he "bumped into" them as he was passing by. The witness he gave grew out of their natural encounter and exchange. Think of the most memorable of those experiences, and it becomes evident: the woman at the well in Samaria (John 4:1-42), the Gadarene demoniac (Mark 5:1-20), the woman who touched the hem of his garment (Matt. 9:20-22), and the meeting of Zaccheus (Luke 19:1-28). Jesus never had to go out of his way to find opportunity; it was *wayside* witnessing. The truth is, we don't have to go out of our way to witness; we meet enough people *in the way!*

Third, witnessing, in our time, must include the *target group* strategy. This is especially true in church programming for evangelism. We are seeing an almost unprecedented sociological phenomenon today in group patterns which must affect our evangelistic methods. Always before the sociological trend has been toward assimilation and integration when migration occurs. The European groups which came to America lived in ghetto fashion for a while, but assimilation into the greater community always followed. Now, however, the trend is reversing! Groups are now regrouping. The reason for it is largely the quest for identity. There is little to lend itself to individuality in our computer-card society, and now ethnic and racial groups are regrouping for personal and individual identity by way of some group. They are resurrecting speech and dress patterns and in some cases even inventing them.

Another affecting factor is that the housing trend of the future is rental. Right now more than half of the housing being built in America is *rental*. And the trend within this housing is toward *specific groups:* singles housing and retirement centers, for example. But, aside from the reasons for it, the implications of it are important to our future evangelistic programs. This is going to require a specialized, "target-group" strategy rather than our present general approach.

TARGET GROUP EVANGELISM

PARENTHETICALLY SPEAKING, we are experimenting with this strategy of "target groups" both in the Yokefellows and in the church program at Heritage, and with enough success to validate it. Our "Uncommons" group is one example. (This is our career-singles group.) "Career-singles" are "different" in many ways. That is, they are usually "orphans" in the church program. Most churches do not have enough of them for a separate "department" and they are shuffled into either the college or young couples groups, where they don't "belong." Then, their *schedules* are different. Being single, often away from home and financially enabled, the weekends are frequently spent away on trips home or weekend excursions. Also, they have a different set of needs, especially *social* needs. Thus, their life-patterns are "uncommon" with others—hence, their name at Heritage.

The traditional response to them, however, has been to say: "You must fit our schedule and our structure" even though they don't fit! Why not let the church exist *for them* rather than the reverse? Why not major on *ministering to them* rather than trying to get them to *fit our existing schedules and structures?* The church must meet them at *their* points of need and on *their* schedules!

Every community today is really a "collection of groups": youth, alcoholics, divorcees, senior citizens, language groups, drug addicts, young parents, etc., etc., ad infinitum. Witnessing, *today,* must take this factor into account. Thus far, we have attempted this approach in a number of ways: the uncommons, childless couples, alcoholics, families with delinquent children and young mothers. Only one has failed and that was due to our inability to completely grasp and understand the point of need. (But, we live in a time when it is a greater sin to sit by and do nothing than it is to get up and make a mistake!) In group ministry, a vital "clue" is being able to see the "groups" within the community.

The retreat was climaxed after dinner with a "celebration" of commitment. In this case, it had to do with our inner lives of devotion and our outer lives of witness. But, this one was different. Usually, a "commitment" takes the form of a personal or private prayer meeting, an "altar call" or something akin to them. The Yokefellow in charge of the commitment service startled the group, however, with a different approach. She asked us to go into the woods around the retreat center and to bring back a piece of God's nature which represented where we were and where we were commiting ourselves to go in terms of our devotional lives and witnessing! Our explanations of our choices would be the "commitment service!"

It, too, was a BREAKTHROUGH! Paradoxically, its impact was like both "Manresa" and "Pine Lane." That is, Pine Lane was a "quiet" BREAKTHROUGH, deep and almost wordless. Manresa, on the other hand, was a "jubilant" experience at the encounter of Christ the *Person.* But, "Manresa II" combined the best of both. It had a quiet element along with the jubilant. It was "deep" and deeply moving, but the indescribable group joy was also obvious. One by one they came with their "visual commitments" from nature.

One was a *weed!* Not a thoroughbred nor a hybrid; just "a weed," she said. But, weeds are necessary and, more importantly, seem to be able to grow *anywhere.* Her "excuse" had been that her schedule and duties had "prevented" her devotional life and witnessing. But, since she was a "weed" anyhow, she realized that she could grow anywhere. That was her commitment.

Another was a piece of *driftwood*. His Christian life was thereby depicted: *just drifting*. His commitment: a *disciplined* life of devotions and witness!

Yet another brought a *budding flower*. It was still in the bud, unbloomed. That was her Christian life of witness. Her devotional life was good, good enough to produce the bud. But, the bloom of her witness had not yet come. It would now!

One other was a *rock*. His explanation: just a stationary piece of the environment! It did not act, sing, move, make a noise, bloom. Nothing! That was his Christian life. But, no more!

That it was a BREAKTHROUGH was evident to everyone present. Our prayer which followed left no doubt. *Giant* steps were taken.

It became evident to the whole church the next morning. As the invitation was extended following the sermon, a young girl came making public her acceptance of Christ as Lord. She sat on the front pew and I knelt in front of her, talking to her about the significance of it, about her desire for baptism and church membership. When I had finished, I stood up—to find myself surrounded by twenty-five or so Yokefellows!

One of them was carrying a large box containing rocks, driftwood, flowers and weeds! The symbols of their commitments!

Notes

1. My contribution to the morning's program was the substance of Chapter 6 of *The Idea of the Laity* on "The Inner Life."

2. "Moving from the Inside Out," Keith Miller. A cassette tape recorded by Creative Resources, Waco: Word, Inc., 1972.

3. See *Renew My Church*, Chapter 5 and *The Idea of the Laity*, Chapter 11.

9. EVERY MOUNTAIN HAS FOUR VALLEYS

A great door and effectual is opened unto me, but there are many adversaries (1 Cor. 16:9, KVJ).

Nineteen hundred seventy-two. How does a pastor "feel" after five years of renewal effort in an existing church? Perhaps it can best be expressed by "holy tiredness." It had been a *long* five years.

Somewhere in that five years I had come to the conclusion that the "answer" for renewal in an existing church lay in developing *parallel programs*. There were those who felt secure within the existing structures and there were those for whom the existing structures were really "strictures"—restricting them in growth and service. Yet, both of these were *loyal* attitudes coming from people who actually loved one another! Thus, we embarked on a "parallel program" approach. At the time, I did not realize the amount of work it was to entail.

By 1972, we were operating two "Sunday Schools." One was the traditional approach and one was built around survey courses in the Bible, Christian History, Ethics, and Theology. We were also operating two approaches to local group ministry. One was the traditional Woman's Missionary Union-Brotherhood programs of the denomination; the other was a system of Yokefellow groups. Likewise, our Church Training program had been refocused: toward specific needs and interests for adults, "learning-doing" for the youth, and the regular program for children. And, our Sunday night format had moved from a monological preaching service to programs of encouragement and celebration led by the laity.

This, in turn, produced more work! A major cause of it was the lack of resource materials for most of what we were doing. This placed an added responsibility upon Willard Wild and me to devise the programs and locate (or develop) the curriculum materials. (See Appendixes B and C.) Then, there was the problem of administration, trying to keep parallel programs going simultaneously, developing record systems and the like. But, the results were gratifying!

Yet, it was five long years in the making. *Five years!* Frankly, it took longer than I had anticipated. And, therein is a profound lesson. The latest statistics for Baptists indicate that the average length of a pastor's ministry in a given church is presently about *half* as long as it takes!

PASTORAL TURNOVER

PARENTHETICALLY SPEAKING, the pastor is usually looked upon by the pulpit committee (notice the singling out of one function, an irony in light of what they expect in addition to his pulpit duties) as a man with a panacea for all their problems. And, the unspoken but statistically verifiable evidence is that they will give him about two and one-half years to accomplish it! He has a program and they agree to underwrite it. He is to be the man with the answers. While he is doing it, he is also to visit, counsel, preach, teach, administer, build buildings, raise funds, prepare bulletins and newsletters, marry, bury, motivate, and be active in civic affairs, the local ministerium, and the denomination!

Of course, this kind of expectation means *the pastor is not on tenure, but on the merit system!* If his preaching, programming, promoting, and personality do not produce the promised panacea—"they" know what to do! Within a one-week period recently, I counseled a young pastor one year out of seminary who was leaving the ministry a broken man; put his wife in contact with a psychiatrist; received a call from one pastor and a letter from another—both classmates of mine and both seeking secular employment. "They" are running us off and "we" are leaving at the rate of ten thousand a year in the United States! Called to do one thing and forced to do another, burdened with unauthorized assignments and wearied by the schedule, we are now face-to-face with the truth that, as Thomas Mullen said, we have the men fit for the ministry, but not a ministry fit for the men! Somehow, we have to learn what to do with each other after two and a half years—besides separating.

This realization allowed me to "slow down" in the process. It was already obvious that change which is *forced* upon a people before they *want* to change is not "change". at all. It is usually *unchanged* quickly. It was then that I began to make it obvious that I intended to *stay*. This allowed me to accept their pace and freed them from the concern that, having started all of this, I might leave them not knowing how to carry it on. Coming as it did about midway in the five years, it actually increased the speed of renewal in the second half!

But, it was not easy being the pastor of one church and *two* programs! And that has its pressures, particularly the constant pressure to stay ahead and yet to be a part of a church in motion. Surprisingly enough, the major pressures did not come from the church, other than the workload which I voluntarily assumed. The greatest pressures came (1) from within myself and (2) from my peers!

Myself! There were times when I had to wrestle with myself during that five years. Times when I thought it would be easier to rekindle the traditional fire rather than build another. Times when I wondered if it was worth it—the time, the effort, the work. Times when I wondered if they saw or cared about the significance of it. But, mostly, the problem-with-myself centered around the pastoral role.

There was not a day during that five years that I did not live with the thought that I was not living up to the expectations of some of the members. The commitment to a ministry of renewal had its own set of implications. One was that as long as I did for them, they would never do it! A pastor's job, in a sense, is to work himself out of a job. *He is to equip them to do the work of the ministry.* The problem was that when I stopped and before they started, there was a "lag" in which it was not being done at all! And that's a hard thing to go to sleep with for five years. Whether they did nor not, I thought that they thought that I was not doing my job. There were times, many times, when I wanted to run for the cover of the conventional. It would have been easier. But, I was committed in another direction.

Along with this fear was a doubt. (They seem to go together, don't they?) The doubt was: *Will it every really work?* The idea of the ministry of the laity? Sunday after Sunday, I looked out from the pulpit at a congregation now grown to over 500 worshippers. Of them, less than 150 were involved in renewal to *any* degree, however meager. Of these, less than half were in the Yokefellow groups, with the balance "making it on their own" in the deeper life of devotion and the wider life of ministry. And, that was at the end of *five years!* Two things, however, kept me at it—whether it would work or not. One was that it was the New Testament's idea, not mine. The second was that I was seeing it work in *some* of their lives. So, I kept at it.

My peers! One staggering realization which came to me early in the effort was that "deviation equals suspicion" among a goodly number of the pastoral fellowship. And, I began to "feel" it almost immediately. My emphasis on *conversion* as a "call to ministry," as opposed to a choice to escape hell without requirements in this life, brought an immediate drop in "baptisms." For one who had always had a fair ratio of annual baptisms to report, this aroused the suspicion among some that, whatever renewal was, it was not "evangelistic." Whatever defense I made on the grounds of the New Testament—that Christ calls us, not to an isolated decision, but to a life of disciplined obedience or that Christ never hid his scars to win a disciple—had little or no effect. *The numbers, where were the numbers?* That was their response.

Then, when we began to alter the "program," it worsened! I remember speaking at an annual associational meeting on one occasion on the subject of "Christian Education." I spoke of the obvious ineffectiveness of the present educational approach and of the possibilities of the survey approach as it was being done at Heritage. Although I was an invited guest speaking on an assigned topic in a distant association, after the service only *two* people spoke to me! Both were laymen who were pleased, but I could not help but notice them looking over their shoulders to see if their pastors were watching. (And, my honorarium arrived three months late and had been reduced by half!)

The pressure came at the point of *acceptance* by my peers. There is an unwritten code of loyalty which every pastor should enjoy among fellow pastors. He not only desires it, he *needs* it, for it is a lonely work at best. And, its absence is a heavy load to bear. I was not *saying* the right things nor *producing* the right statistics nor *promoting* the right programs. But, not without cost. It was not outright ostracism for everyone still "spoke." But, there was that obvious air of suspicion about my "not being one of us." My closest friends in the ministry were, for the most part, of other denominations for a good while. And, my Baptist friends were a scattered lot, throughout the States, mostly those involved in some form of renewal.

I came to see, however, that the problem was the same one I had faced, a sense of insecurity and fear. I knew it well! And, it allowed a measure of freedom and acceptance on my part. As time passed, however, I began to find myself being sought out by others asking "what we were doing" at Heritage and indicating the desire for it where they were. That kept me going, too. That they always did it privately made me wonder, though. Yet, across those five years, the fellowship began to grow and we met periodically for support and discussion. But, we were few, at best.

The "saving salt" in this era of suspicion was my unquestionable loyalty to the denomination. Were it not for that, the Heritage experiment could well have been written off as "separatist" or "independent." Yet, we were giving 25 percent of our offerings to the denominational program; I was serving on state and national denominational committees; and we were unashamedly open in our loyalty and commitment to the denomination. Try as anyone could, they could not evade that!

In spite of all that was going on at the church in terms of renewal, there were low moments, *personal* low moments. And, I want to be honest in my report of it. Dealing with myself and my peers frequently brought me low, very low. As best as I knew, I was trying to be loyal to my calling; I was trying to grow an effective church of committed ministers; I was giving every evidence of my denominational loyalty; I was trying to love and encourage, to be creative and effective—and what we were doing was *working*. But, acceptance came slowly: five long years *within* the church; and *outside* the church—well, that was obvious.

Were it not for the *results*, however meager, those five years would have been enough, more than enough. But, there were some observable results. Statistically, it was evident. We were growing . . . in and with change. Our annual reports indicate a part of it.

	Total Members	Resident Members	Total New Members	Offerings	Mission Gifts*
1968	1254	822	97	$61,858	$12,313
1969	1257	825	55	$69,483	$15,599
1970	1277	845	65	$70,644	$16,952
1971	1307	875	67	$77,546	$18,376
1972	1337	905	65	$89,897**	$23,559

* This does not include some $3000 in stipends and services provided annually for the student program.
** This does not include an additional $46,500 given by the members during 1972 toward the building in a special offering.

Some of the most encouraging elements could not be "reported," however: There was no blank on the form for them! Elements like inner growth, a sense of ministry discovered, the many of those 1,337 who had been "reclaimed," and the growth in Sunday attendance from 400 to 600 in the morning service. The records did indicate a most significant gain: *stewardship*. The percentage of increase in giving was double that of the percentage of increase in new members![1] I am convinced that, in our time, there is no greater hurdle to cross in the Christian life than *greed*. We are a money-oriented culture. And a good index to one's growth in

Christ, if not one of the best, is *giving!* Heritage was *growing*.

STEWARDSHIP

PARENTHETICALLY SPEAKING, this financial growth is, in itself, a miracle story in that it took place without the usual "promotion" which accompanies church financial programs. We do not have an annual "budget promotion" at Heritage! The budget is presented in November of each year without promotion. In January or February, we have a "Stewardship Education" emphasis. That is, we try to couch stewardhip, not in terms of giving to support a cause or a budget, but rather in terms of what the Christ expects of each of us. We do not "whip up" support of a budget; rather we call for personal commitment apart from any budget or program. These are two different things!

Our "Stewardship Education" consists of a Sunday School lesson on the biblical principles of giving and sometimes a sermon on tithing. Our "pledge cards," which do not call for a pledge, are mailed with a message and thoughts on "giving." There is no house-to-house canvas, no follow-up, no promotion. The card indicates that it is an "estimate" of giving and there is no place for a name on it. There is no "parade" of bringing cards to the front during a service, no class or department goals, not even a church goal! Yet, it works!

The idea is to put the responsibility on the individual in terms of *personal stewardship*. The most indicative thing on the card is the question: "Does this represent an increase over last year?" That's the clue to true stewardship!

The report on "baptisms," approximately thirty or so per year, is not so encouraging, however. There is a partial explanation for a lower than usual ratio, and it is not due to a lack of evangelistic emphasis! A major part of it is the content of the "invitation" at Heritage: commitment. There is no "watering down" of the call of Christ to a *life* of *disciplined commitment*. He did not call for admirers; He called for laborers. He was more interested in *disciples* than *decisions*. His emphasis was on *what* they were "deciding"! (Perhaps this play on "decisions verses disciples" is mere semantics. To be sure, a decision is required. The Christian life begins with a choice, a decision. The stress here is being given to making sure that the "content" of the decision—to become a disciple—is made clear to all concerned.) Were they deciding that they did not want to go to hell? that they "appreciated" Christ dying for them? that they were glad they would not have to answer for their sins? Or, were they deciding that, for the rest of their lives, they would make Jesus "Lord" of their lives? A mere "decision" is beside the point, apart from the *content* of it. Jesus knew it well. On one occasion, He asked: "What do you think? A man had two sons; and he went to the first and said, 'Son, go and work in the vineyard today.' And he answered, 'I will not'; but afterward he repented and went. And he went to the second and said the same; and he answered, 'I go, sir,' but did not go. Which of the two did the will of his father?" (Matt. 21:28-31). What do *you* think? At Heritage, statistics or no, we have tried to be faithful at the point of explaining *what* Christ wants in the way of followers, and that has had its effect!

Another element is the conclusion shared by a growing number of us in Heritage that God does not necessarily want everyone to belong to Heritage Church! In fact, he doesn't even want everyone to be a Baptist! Our task is not to "get members"; rather, it is to help others find Christ and then to find his will for *their* lives. That "will" may not include our church! Consequently, a goodly number of those won out in the world by Heritage witnesses end up in other churches, a number perhaps equal to those who do join.

But, this does not fully explain nor defend it. The truth is, it represents the major failure in our efforts toward renewal. True renewal is always evangelistic; if we are "renewed," we are witnesses, or we are not "renewed." The foregoing chapters relate our problems and attempts at witnessing and we are presently on the verge of it. I expect it to be the next BREAKTHROUGH—witnessing on an "as you go" basis.

But, candor demands the public confession that baptismal statistics, however sacred they may be to any group, do not represent the standard by which God judges us. His standard is *faithfulness to assigned tasks.* Consequently, we refuse to bow before the "altar" of statistical success. I know very well how to get more "decisions"!

Christ, however, called us "to make disciples" and that means being honest about that to which Christ invites others through us: *discipleship*. Experience thus far indicates that this has fewer "takers," but they *stay!* And, that's the real test. (I have often thought that the reporting of "baptisms" would be more accurate if it was done . . . five years later!) If renewal means anything at all to Christianity, it is a renewed emphasis on the *integrity* of church membership and the integrity of *evangelism*, too. Christians must be *faithful* to Christ first and *acceptable* to others later. Besides, "acceptance" is *their choice, not ours.*

Yet, 1972, for all its mixed blessings and confusing emotions, represented just that: *acceptance!* And, when it started, it flooded! In 1972 . . .

. . . our new building, dedicated March 5, built around renewal concepts, won the "Honor Award" for architecture at the triennial church architect's conference in Nashville!

. . . that same day, March 5, *Renew My Church*, was publicly introduced and, in the first eighteen months, won "acceptance" by 10,000 readers!

. . . my Baptist alma mater, Georgetown College, named me as one of the "Outstanding Alumni" of 1972 for my renewal activities!

. . . speaking engagements came from all across the nation and Europe; from churches, pastor's conferences, state evangelism clinics, and they were mostly among *Baptists!*

. . . and, at long last, our denomination entered into "renewal" through the appointment of directors at both the Home Mission Board and the Brotherhood Commission!

And, that is a . . . BREAKTHROUGH! For *all* of us!

Notes

1. This continued to be the pattern in 1973 when our offerings went from $89,897 to $106,858 and our missions giving from $23,599 to $27,585.

10. WHERE NEXT, FOR CHRIST'S SAKE?

Where there is no vision, the people perish (Prov. 29:18, KJV).

At this writing, the fall of 1973, the renewal experiment at the Heritage Baptist Church in Annapolis stands at the beginning of its seventh year. It has brought many changes, but not merely "change for the sake of change." Rather, it has been an attempt to *actualize* the lay ministry concept of the New Testament in the context of an existing church. Our "goal" has been an *emerging* goal; that is, it has grown as we have journeyed. But, the *vision* of it is still our magnificent obscession!

It is a vision of a group of people who are, first of all, committed to Jesus Christ as the Lord of their individual and collective lives and who, simultaneously, are as committed to each other as they are to Christ. (This is the step from an *ekklesia*, an assembly, to a *koinonia*, a fellowship.) It is the vision of a people who have not so much "joined" the fellowship as they have been "brought" to it by the Holy Spirit because they have "gifts" which complete the Body in terms of its various functions. The Spirit brings them not only because they *have* gifts, but because they *are* gifts and he "gives" them to the others. In the vision, the warmth of their *koinonia* fellowship creates the environmental conditions which allow those gifts to emerge and then the corporate fellowship provides for the equipping of the person to exercise their gifts in the ministry of Christ to others. (This is the step from *koinonia* to *diakonia*, ministry.) In turn, some of these gifts are employed within the fellowship in the equipping and encouraging of still other members. Some are carried on outside the church. These gifts, however, are not merely "good things" to do; rather they are *Christ's* assignments. (This is the difference in *lay involvement* and *lay ministry.*) Some of it is done alone while some of it is done as a group effort with others of similar callings and gifts. The end result is a concerted effort, in the power of the Holy Spirit, to minister to the needs of both the fellowship and the world as Christ leads. Such was and is the vision.

Along with that vision, however, we also *see it as it is!* In *existing* churches, some have not been "brought" to the fellowship. They have "joined" it, and not always for the best of reasons. In *existing* churches, some are not committed to Christ as *Lord.* Indeed, many are barely committed to him as Savior! Nor are many of them *functioning* parts of the Body. And, of those who are, many are not "exercising their gifts" so much as they are "filling a position" or "doing a job." In *existing* churches, there is an observable absence of commitment to each other in terms of *agape* love and, consequently, *concerted* effort is a luxury. In *existing* churches, many have no inner life of devotion and the "power of the Spirit" is but a phrase rather than an experienced reality. They are "self-led" rather than Christ-followers and frequently are simply "pushed" by emotional and environmental factors. In short, the "as-is" is a far cry from the vision of renewal in existing churches.

How, then, do we get from *here* to *there?* One answer is: We can't! If this is true, that the hope for renewal among existing churches is a waterless cloud, then we have several options. We can quit entirely: just give up on the "church" idea. Or, we can accept the church as it is and "live" with it. Or, finally, we can break away and form a "new" church, leaving the others to struggle with the problems we helped to create.

The other answer is: Christ can! We cannot give up on the "church" idea; it is not *our* idea! It is *his!* True, the church is presently less than he intended, but even that is a basic clue to renewal! To be "less than Christ intends" is the essential definition of . . . *sin!* "For all have sinned, and *come short* of the glory of God (Rom. 3:23, italics added). If we view the present state of the church as a *sin* against God, we are en route to renewal simply because we cannot "accept" sin as being acceptable to him! While the admission of it is a breaking experience and while the challenges of renewal are unimaginably difficult, he is still the *Savior* from sin! *He* can do it. He *is* doing it!

The foregoing is one report of how it is coming about in one existing congregation, a congregation which is refusing to stay and daring to follow him. It has been a long, yet delight-filled journey and both God and we know that we are still en route, some in the Yokefellow groups and some by way of the (renewed) traditional. At the beginning of this seventh year, Heritage is vastly different than we were seven years ago. Should you attend a Sunday morning worship service, you would probably miss it. But, behind the scenes and at other times—there it is real and evident.

On Sunday morning, at 9:15 A.M., two Sunday Schools are going on with indepth study of the Bible, Christian History, Ethics, and doctrine.

On Sunday night, at 6:00 P.M., you would be likely to find a seminar on the Christian Family or Christian Black Studies or Transactional Analysis. And at 7:00 P.M. you would probably share in a service led by lay people or a celebration led by the youth.

Throughout the week and the month, you would be able to see . . .

    An evangelistic Bible study group (first Friday)
    A Yokefellow One Meeting (first Saturday)
    A Couples Sharing Group (first-third Friday)
    A Childless Couples Sharing Group (each Tuesday)
    A Career-Singles Group (Sunday morning)
    A Family Therapy Group (Thursday night)
    A Ladies Bible Study (Tuesday morning)
    A State Hospital Ministry Group (Thursday morning)
    A Ladies Visitation Group (Tuesday morning)
    A Yokefellow Two Meeting (third Friday)
    A Prayer Group (second-fourth Friday night)

A Drop-In Prayer Meeting (Friday morning)

Likewise, you would see WMU "mission action" projects and ministries, done in the context of the traditional structures; deacons trying to actualize their ministries as spiritual leaders of the congregation; and teens actually "Christing-it" among their friends.

And, in Annapolis, Baltimore, and Washington, you would find a cadre of ministers . . . not doing good things, but Christ's things . . . in an unapologetic fashion. And, we believe it has really just begun! (This emphasis on the various group belies the *total* picture of church, a regrettable feature with which the writer has wrestled all the way through the book. That is, "renewal" is not "groups," per se; it is the idea of *ministry*. More often than not, this includes existing structures and methods as well as the new. There are a great many in renewal at Heritage who are not in the groups.)

And not just with us! In the last two years a new door has opened to our Yokefellows and, consequently, various teams of us have shared in church meetings, lay renewal weekends, retreats and pastor's conferences in Maryland, District of Columbia, North Carolina, Virginia, New Jersey, West Virginia, Georgia, Texas, Ohio, Indiana, Louisiana, and California. One of them is typical. The Sunday School teacher of a young couples class in another state heard me speak at a conference in yet another state. He asked if I would come and share the Yokefellow idea with his class. I said no but that I would bring a group of Yokefellows and let *them* speak! A date was set and a group of ten met with some twenty-five members of the class for one full Saturday. Three months later, we received a note from them that they had started a Yokefellow group and were meeting once a month, studying *Renew My Church*. Six months later, another note came. They were now averaging thirty-six at their meetings, were beginning some small group ministries—and *would I come and speak to their deacons* since the teacher had become the chairman?

Added to this are the reports of lay renewal weekends led by lay men and women trained and directed through the Brotherhood Commission and the Home Mission Board of our denomination, the efforts of various state conventions (Texas and Louisiana, in particular), and the work of such Baptist-related groups as Lay

Ministries, Inc. (Box 1204, Arlington, Tx. 76010) and the Evangelism Research Foundation (900 N. Dairy Ashford Road, Houston, Tx. 77024). And since Christ's Church is broader than the Baptists, we must see the results of the lay movement in other denominations and in groups like Faith at Work (1000 Century Plaza, Columbia, Md. 21043), the Institute of Church Renewal (1610 LaVista Road, N.E., Atlanta, Ga. 30329) and Yokefellows (230 College Ave., Richmond, Ind. 47374). And, it's just begun!

As the horizon widens before us at Heritage, a number of unmet needs and becoming challenges are still beckoning.

1. *Within Heritage.* There are a great many in the Heritage circle who still have not discovered their gifts and, hence, their reason for existence. We shall continue to reach out within!

2. *Evangelism.* Already mentioned (chapter 9), the spreading of the Word is and shall be our priority business but without either the attitudes or the pace of "business-as-usual." In a land where 60 percent of the population will not come to church, evangelism must be done *out there* in the world. This means the *laity* is our only hope. They must be taught to witness "as they go." It also means focusing in on target groups. At this writing, we are working on the premise of adding two new target groups each year. This year it is "alcoholics" and "the retarded." Next? We do not know, but, God does.

3. *New Members.* It has been our attempt to link new members with the two Yokefellow groups, but even this is an inadequate approach. It is inadequate in that the introduction to the idea of lay ministry is a slow process this way, once per month. While this is better than nothing, the challenge before us is the development of renewal curriculum materials. Existing materials of this nature simply do not deal with the lay ministry ideas of the New Testament. Rather, they tend to deal more with the location of denominational offices and a fragmented approach to prayer, Bible study, etc., apart from the total perspective of ministry. We want to work on this.

4. *Youth Renewal.* Similar in need to new members is that of the youth group: renewal training. There is a great deal of material and resources for exciting and encouraging teenagers in Christ,

but an almost total absence of anything geared to introducing them to the idea of ministry apart from "good things."

Our renewal program to date has centered primarily on *adults* and, more specifically, on adults *already in the church*. This was the place to begin. But, the next step at Heritage (indeed, in the whole renewal movement) is to expose teenagers to the concept before adulthood, saving the task of having to "un-do" before "doing" as with adults.

5. *Retirees.* By 1985 fully 21.2 million people will retire between the ages of fifty-five and sixty-four. Many industrial plants now have the "thirty years and out" retirement plan in effect, regardless of age. (One man I know, employed by a General Motors division, will retire this year at the age of fifty-two!) The military also retires after twenty and thirty years. One can only touch the hem of imagination's garment as to the potential for Christian ministry among and by this group. These people are, for the most part, physically healthy, mentally keen, and financially independent. Businessmen could become church business managers; teachers could become religious education directors; there is no reason why there could not be a complete retooling for a person to a church-related ministry. And, most of it could be done with little or no remuneration by the churches since most of these persons already have adequate retirement income! Heretofore, our thought has been to entertain these able-bodied and willing men and women. But why not equip and engage them in ministry?

And, on and on we could go with this sampling of the more obvious "unfinished business" before us. But, it is still only the beginning!

The most difficult, if not impossible, task of this present report is . . . where to end it. Because it has no end. It is but . . . an *interim report* . . . of our BREAKTHROUGH!

"Now to him who by the power at work within us is able to do far more abundantly than all that we ask or think, to him be glory in the church and in Christ Jesus to all generations, for ever and ever. Amen" (Eph. 3:20-21).

EPILOGUE

Now you have observed my teaching, my conduct, my aim in life, my faith, my patience, my love, my steadfastness, my persecutions and my sufferings (2 Tim. 3:10-11).

How does one get started with the renewal process (and it is a *process*) in an *existing church? Is there a pattern, an approach to it? I think so. At least an outline. While the subpoints may vary, the outline is fairly obvious. It comes in stages.*

STAGE ONE—INVESTIGATION

The process begins with one, preferably the pastor, capturing the concept of renewal. Just one. Jesus appealed to the lukewarm church at Laodicea by saying, "If anyone hears my voice [just one] and opens the door, I will come in" (Rev. 3:20). Let's assume that *you* are to be that one!

The "concept of renewal" has to do with (1) the *deeper life* of devotion and (2) the *wider life* of lay ministry. There should be a period in which one investigates it until he captures the concept, or perhaps, is captured by it. As important as knowing what it is, is knowing what it is not. That is, the deeper life is not a periodic, emotional booster-shot as "revivals" have sometimes been mistakenly used. Rather, it is a life lived out in the power, and under the control, of the Spirit of Christ. The difference is that of a *quiet constancy*.

Likewise, the *universal ministry* (that all believers are in the ministry) does not refer to church members getting busier, doing more "church work" (which is not always the same as the "work of the church"), or finding good things to do. Rather, it is the discovery of each believer's gifts and ministries and then fulfilling them. The *equipping ministry* of the pastor, by the same token, is not the people doing all the work. Rather, it is him helping them find the Lord's work for them to do, training them to do it, and encouraging them as they follow through. (And, believe me, this requires more time than doing it yourself!)

Your "capturing the concept" also includes studying various "models" of how renewal looks once it is underway. This will require your reading of the reports and, if possible, visiting those places where it is going on.

This investigation stage for you, then, includes grasping the deeper life, the lay- and equipping-ministry, and seeing the existing expressions of it. It will not come overnight, however; it is a radical reorientation of both your thinking and behavioral patterns. And that takes *time!* Remember, renewal is a *process;* it is far more than either an experience or an announcement.

Below are some suggested books for you to read. (Reading and renewal seem to be inseparable teammates!) It is suggested that they be read together. Read one book from each of the three sections before reading the second book in any one section. All of these are available at local religious book stores.

The Deeper Life
Journey into Fullness, James Mahoney
On Beginning from Within, Douglas Steere
Life on the Highest Plane, Ruth Paxon
A Testament of Devotion, Thomas Kelly

The Universal Ministry
The Renewal of the Ministry, Thomas Mullen
Renew My Church, David Haney
The Greening of the Church, Findley Edge
The Company of the Committed, Elton Trueblood
The Idea of the Laity, David Haney

The Existing Models
The Seven Last Words of the Church, Ralph Neighbour
Brethren, Hang Loose, Robert Girard
Call to Commitment, Elizabeth O'Connor
The Touch of the Spirit, Ralph Neighbour
A New Face for the Church, Larry Richards
The Emerging Church, Larson & Osborne

This is by no means an exhaustive list, but it contains reports and perspectives suitable and adaptable to all evangelical congregations.

STAGE TWO—*INTERPRETATION*

Having captured the concept and then being captured by it by deliberate decisions to actualize it in your own life and ministry, begin to share the story with others.

For a pastor, this could include preaching on the themes of renewal: a series on the deeper life and one on the universal ministry, using the existing models for illustrative matter. This could also be done in special classes, in prayer meeting or an elective Church Training seminar. It could be incorporated into existing group agendas: a "study time" in the deacons' meeting or church council meeting, or used on retreats for these groups. These could take the shape of the pastor sharing out of his pilgrimage or the study of a book together. (The writer's *Renew My Church* and *The Idea of the Laity* were written with this in mind.) Many of the books listed previously are adaptable to this use. Or, the church could have a "congregational reading program" with the whole congregation reading a book on renewal during a specified period, followed by a dialogue-study of the ideas. The pastor could also give books to particular people, urging them to read the books and then (equally important) talking with them later about the books and the peoples reactions to them.

For a layman, this sharing of the story could take place in a Sunday School class. One teacher I know used the monthly class meeting for this purpose. Whatever is done, however, should be shared with the pastor. If the pastor is unaware of the nature of renewal, there may be some valid apprehension on his part. Care should be exercised to inform him as to exactly what is meant by "renewal." While you may be saying "renewal," he may be hearing "tongues" and when you say "groups," he may hear "cliques." A good approach to this problem might be giving him a copy of Thomas Mullen's book, *The Renewal of the Ministry* (on the "equipping ministry") or Findley Edge's *The Greening of the Church*.

But, spread the word to other Christians within the church. By so doing, you will create the hunger for "the more" that Christ has in mind.

Together, the stages of *investigation* and *interpretation* will require six months to a year. At least, that is the report of most churches in the process.

STAGE THREE—*INITIATION*

It is more and more obvious that before renewal can breathe new life into a congregation, there must be an initiating *event*. This is when the concept is gathered up from the various interpretation clusters (the deacons, church council, study groups, etc.), and forcefully presented to the *total* church as an alternative. To be sure, the renewal perspective will never be churchwide; most likely it will never include all of the members in any church. Some of them just do not care and others are not interested. But, some are interested, some do care, and some will "see it" and embark on their journeys. The way to initiate it is with an event. This can take any number of forms.

1. *Lay Renewal Weekend.* The Lay Renewal Weekend (also called Lay Witness Weekend or Lay Witness Mission) is one of the most effective ways of initiating renewal on a churchwide basis. It is simply a group of outside lay people coming into church for a weekend of sharing. Under the direction of a trained coordinator, it usually involves a Friday night church dinner followed by small group meetings led by the witnesses. These gather in various rooms throughout the building and, after getting acquainted, each shares where he or she "is." The witnesses stay in the homes of members that evening, again sharing, and Saturday morning features home gather-

ings of small groups led by the witnesses. Saturday night is like the Friday night meetings without the dinner. On Sunday morning, the witnesses lead in the Sunday School hour and, then, two or three speak in the morning service. The almost unanimous report is that these weekends are *miracles* in terms of commitments made and journeys begun!

To have one requires outside help, however. The Southern Baptist Convention provides this through a joint effort of the Home Mission Board and the Brotherhood Commission. For information, contact: Reid Hardin, HMB Division of Evangelism, 1350 Spring Street, Atlanta, Georgia, 30309 or Brotherhood Commission, 1548 Poplar Avenue, Memphis, Tennessee 38104. Another group during these weekends, providing either all Baptist lay witnesses or a mixed denominational group, is Lay Ministries, Inc., P. O. Box 1204, Arlington, Texas, 76010. Some churches find that by having Methodists, Presbyterians, and others in the group is even more effective, and Lay Ministries, Inc. is able to do this. (On their Advisory Board are such Baptist leaders as: Owen Cooper, former SBC President, Dr. Cal Guy, Dr. Findley Edge, and Leonard Holloway.) Yet another group, Methodist-oriented, is the Institute of Church Renewal, the originator of the lay witness weekend concept (1610 LaVista Road, N.E., Atlanta, Georgia, 30329).

2. *Deeper Life Conference.* A Deeper Life Conference (or "Inner Life," "Spiritual Life"), is similar to a "revival" in that it is a week of preaching-teaching. The object of such, however, is the introduction of the idea of the Spirit-controlled life and a call to commitment for Christians. This was the approach used at Heritage Church.

3. *Church Renewal Conference.* A Church Renewal Conference is similar to the above Deeper Life Conference, but it also includes the outer-life of ministry idea along with the inner-life emphasis. In these meetings are also included some dialogue sessions with the speaker and lay guests involved in renewal and the presentation of some "models." The result is an *overview* of the total renewal process, coupled with a call to commitment. This approach is being used effectively

and often speeds up the process by presenting the total picture at the very outset.

4. *Renewal Retreat.* Yet another effective way to initiate renewal is the retreat. This is a time and a place away—at a camp or retreat center—where the renewal ideas can be presented and commitments made. The format can follow any number of patterns, but the objective in this case is the introduction of the ideas of renewal and its initiation. Various renewal books can be studied or it could be a Deeper Life Conference or a Church Renewal Conference, just held at a different location! It also has the added advantage of time for more small group activity than is true of the conference. Its disadvantage is that it has a tendency to reach fewer people even though it may reach them better. This can be led by the pastor or by the pastor and various church leaders; a church can also invite an outside leader.

Another approach to the retreat idea is that of going to a retreat center and utilizing their staff with its expertise. Such places are: The Vineyard Conference Center on the campus of Southern Baptist Theological Seminary in Louisville, led by Findley Edge, Harvey Hester, and William Clemmons; Laity Lodge in Kerrville, Texas; the various Yokefellow Centers— Richmond, Indiana; Shakertown, Kentucky; Defiance, Ohio, and elsewhere.

The writer has been involved in each of these approaches and all hold great promise. The particular method used is best determined locally by whatever best fits the situation. But, someway, the process must be initiated. There is a time of study, then a period of spreading the word and, finally, an event.

STAGE FOUR—*EDUCATION*

The next stage in the process is that of gathering a group out of the event. In each case, whether a weekend, a conference or a retreat, an appeal can be made to those who "might wish to pursue these ideas." Thus, the renewal group is underway! (Indeed, this was the very method of Jesus in gathering disciples and, then, from them, gathering twelve apostles!) A group may already exist, having started during the *interpretation* stage, which could be the nucleus of the on-going group. If not, a new group can start. This can be a try-it-for-eight-weeks group, or it can be started to exist indefinitely.

The Lay Renewal Weekend seems to create more groups; the conferences or retreat, a single core group. It is my opinion, however, that the better approach following the event, is for the pastor to meet with the total group (or groups) to teach, to guide, and to share. Some renewalists are hesitant at the point of pastoral involvement, fearing on one hand that the people will not be as "open" in their sharing with him present or, on the other hand, that he will dominate the meetings. These are possibilities, true; but he is the pastor-teacher-equipper (Eph. 4:11-12) and the position of leadership is one he cannot abdicate. If he understands renewal and if he is aware of group dynamics, there will be no problem; and this is usually the case. In any event, the group shortchanges itself if it does not utilize his expertise in the Bible and theology.

During the initial stages of the group, perhaps for a year or so, the group needs to grapple with the ideas of (1) the deeper life, (2) the concept of ministry, and (3) the nature of *koinonia* fellowship. Our experience at Heritage, which has been confirmed by the reports of others, is that these concepts require more than announcement and definition! It takes a while to soak in! (See chapter 3.)

Also, during this period is the time to teach group dynamics. (See chapter 3). Then, the group (or groups) can handle their own problems.

The shape of this stage, then, would be that of a monthly (or twice monthly) meeting of the total group with the pastor in which they would study together on the ideas of renewal. If the group is large, too large for discussion, the discussion period could be that of breaking into smaller groups which, in turn, report back to the whole group.

Of critical importance during this stage is also that of a "minimum discipline." (See Appendix A). This cannot be emphasized too much!

There will come a time when the group is ready to launch out in small groups, group ministries, and individual ministries. This necessitates the next stage.

STAGE FIVE—*COORDINATION*

Coordination is necessary so long as renewal is viewed as a *church-centered* effort. Remember, it is the *church* which we seek to renew, not individual members *in isolation* or small separatist groups. The members are to edify the Body and the Body is to nourish the members; but, the church is to be a *Body,* a coordinated organism. If this is not the case, then it is not of Christ—if the New Testament is our guide!

The method of coordination will be determined in the local situation under the leadership of the Holy Spirit. The methods given to Heritage Church, and one successfully being used by others, is a good illustration. It is that of the pastor meeting monthly with a cluster of groups which, in turn, meet weekly or twice per month. In our situation, it is two clusters of groups, taking the form of a hub and spokes. (Also see the writer's *The Idea of the Laity,* p. 180.)

Coordination will also become necessary as structural changes become evident, particularly with the educational program of the church and the reordering of responsibilities. Much of this will be done through existing organizations, but some of it will require new ways and methods. And, that requires *coordination*—the alternative to which is *chaos!*

But, how long? How long does it take? The only, but frustrating, answer is: however long it takes! Probably several years. We did not get into our present situation overnight, nor will we emerge from it overnight. Yet, "how long?" is an invalid question. Our call is to begin and to continue. That is our *only* call: "Follow me."

APPENDIXES

Appendix A – The Minimum Discipline

Below is a reproduction of the "Minimum discipline" cards used by the Heritage Yokefellow groups.

A MINIMUM DISCIPLINE

1. *The Discipline of Devotion.* To read a portion of Scripture and to pray each day, preferably in the morning.
2. *The Discipline of Worship.* To share at least once each week in church worship.
3. *The Discipline of Giving.* To share a definite portion of my income in the work of Christ, preferably a tithe.
4. *The Discipline of Study.* To spend time in the reading of Christian books and articles each week.
5. *The Discipline of Ministry.* To discover my ministry and to exercise it faithfully in the power of the Spirit.
6. *The Discipline of Witness.* To share with others, unapologetically, the good news of Christ's ability to save and help.
7. *The Discipline of Fellowship.* To be involved with specific other Christians in an effort of mutual encourgement.

BIBLE READING HELPS

As you read a daily portion of Scripture, ask of it the following questions. Is there . . .

An error to avoid? A duty to perform?
A truth to learn?   A sin to confess?
A prayer to echo?   A promise to claim?

CHRISTIAN READING

The following books are recommended as beginning reading for the Christian. Check each as you read them.

☐ *Renew My Church*
                by David Haney
☐ *Company of the Committed*
                by Elton Trueblood
☐ *The Greening of the Church*
                by Findley Edge
☐ *No Longer Strangers*
                by Bruce Larson
☐ *The Idea of the Laity*
                by David Haney
☐ *Journey Into Fullness*
                by James Mahoney
☐ *The Touch of the Spirit*
                by Ralph Neighbour

Appendix B

Curriculum Materials
for the
Heritage Baptist Church
Annapolis, Maryland

(Adult Sunday School Program)

1. Old Testament: *A Brief Introduction to the Old Testament* by Adam Miller. (Anderson, Indiana: Warner Press, 1964.)
2. Life of Christ: *The Life and Ministry of Our Lord* by Ray Robbins. (Nashville: Convention Press.)
3. Life of Paul: *The Growth of the Early Church* by W. A. Carleton. (Nashville: Convention Press.)
4. Church History: *The Story of the Church* by A. M. Renwick. (Grand Rapids: Eerdman's.)
5. Christian Ethics: *The Christian Life* by Waldo Beach. (Richmond, Va.: The CLC Press.)
6. Christian Doctrine: *The Baptist Faith and Doctrine* by Herschel Hobbs, (Nashville: Convention Press) and/or *Christian Doctrine* by J. S. Whale, (Cambridge University Press, 1941.)
  (This covers a two year cycle, September to June, omitting the summer quarter. All of these are paperbacks.)

Appendix C

Please fill in the blanks and put in the offering plate or hand to Mr. Wild, Miss Myers, or Pastor Haney.

Adult Seminars. We are in the process of planning the 1973-74 adult Training Seminar programs and would like to know your interests. Please check.

- ( ) Family Life
- ( ) Bible Study
- ( ) Cults
- ( ) Devotional Life
- ( ) Regular T.U.
- ( ) Current Issues
- ( ) World Religions
- ( ) Drug Abuse
- ( ) Awareness
- ( ) Teacher Training
- ( ) Race Relations
- ( ) Renewal
- ( ) Other Denominations
- ( ) Witnessing
- ( ) Political Issues
- ( ) Devotional Classics—Augustine, Calvin, St. Francis, etc.
- ( ) Modern Literature—for moral, ethical discussion.
- ( ) Please list any other seminar topic you would like: _____

PERSONAL DYNAMICS. We are considering offering a course on personal dynamics, This would be a 13 session course, using tapes from a professional organization. Designed for leaders (how to work with others, understand them, motivate them), it would be a secular approach, but with carry-over into church and Christian leadership. We are thinking of deacons, teachers, etc., but it would be of value to anyone working with people. There would probably be a minimal charge of $3.00 to $5.00 each.

1. ( ) Interested   ( ) Not Interested
2. ( ) Prefer T.U. hour, 6:00-7:00 on Sunday p.m.
3. ( ) Prefer Wednesday night, 7:30 p.m.
4. ( ) Prefer a "crash," week-long course.

ADULT SUNDAY SCHOOL. After the two-year cycle of special courses, I would prefer a study of. . . . Please check as many as you like.

( ) A study of one book of the Bible, like John or the Psalms. List your choices: _____
( ) A study of a period of church history, like the 1st Century, the Reformation or the Ana-baptists. Any preference? _____
( ) Other: _____

_____   _____
Your Name   Phone Number

Appendix D—Deacon Family Ministries

The materials used in the Deacon Family Ministries program at Heritage are the standard forms of the Baptist Sunday School Board. These may be obtained at any Baptist Book Store (Forms 4333-33, 4333-34, 4333-35, 4333-36).

The deacons also use the following "calling card" in their visiting.

```
┌─────────────────────────────────────────────────────────────┐
│  Deacon Family Ministries          Yoked Together in Christ │
│                                                             │
│               HERITAGE BAPTIST CHURCH                       │
│                    1740 Forest Drive                        │
│                   Annapolis, Md. 21401                      │
│                       263-6680                              │
│                                                             │
│   _____              _____            │
│     Family Deacon                   Telephone               │
└─────────────────────────────────────────────────────────────┘
```

Appendix E—Yokefellow Bible Studies

The following represents the study outline forms used by Yokefellow Two in their study of the "Seven Churches of Asia" (Rev. 1-3). Note the emphasis on the *positive* and the *practical*, particularly noted by the asterisks(*).

Seven Churches of Asia #2   Yokefellow Two Study
THE CHURCH AT SMYRNA
"The Suffering Church"
Rev. 2:8-11

1. What makes a Church rich?
   1.   6.
   2.   7.
   3.   8.
   4.   9.
   5.   10.
2. What makes a *Christian* rich? The same things which make a Church rich. Virtues such as faith, love and service do not exist apart from *persons*, however. If the church to which you belong is to be rich, than *you* must be rich! (Discuss this if you wish.)
3. What makes a church *poor?*
*4. If the Church to which you belong is poor, it is due to *poor* members. Do you contribute to your church's *wealth* or *poverty?* Or both?
5. According to 2:10, how much are you to "take," to endure before you may quit? What does it take to be faithful? What makes the difference in a faithful and an unfaithful Christian? List them.
*6. How can we help each other to be faithful? (Christ is here using the method of "encouraging." How do we encourage others?)

Seven Churches of Asia #4   Yokefellow Two Study
THE CHURCH AT THYATIRA
Thyatira is the smallest of the seven cities, famous for its purple cloth (Lydia of Acts 16:14 was from here) and for its many guilds. The Lord is introduced as the one whose eyes see all and who has feet of bronze, i.e., able to subdue. A lady ("Jezebel"), claiming to be a prophetess, is leading the church astray—probably like the aforementioned Nicolaitans. He Himself will deal with this; the others are to repent or hold fast as the case may be. The overcomers will rule in the end and will be given the morning star, a reference to eternal life and/or Himself.
*1. "I know your works." He commends their *love, faith, service* (ministry) and *patient endurance.* Let each member of your group state what he or she thinks Christ would commend in the lives of the other

group members. Don't be embarrassed if you don't know some of the group and can't say anything.
*2. Notice how Christ "affirms" them: *Your latter works exceed your first.* Discuss the nature of affirming and encouraging by letting each one share . . .
   (1) An encouraging verse of Scripture. Record these to report later.
   (2) The most encouraging person you have known. Let someone record the chief characteristics of these encouragers.
 3. We have previously discussed much of the subject matter of this letter in the previous studies. We have not discussed "repentance" at any length, however. Discuss:
   (1) The meaning (how to) of repenting.
   (2) The implications of the fact that we *can* repent!

THE CHURCH AT LAODICCA
"The Lukewarm Church"

*1. List some *synonyms* for "lukewarm." For instance, "satisfied." Remember, a church is made up of members and if it is lukewarm, it is because the *members* are. Therefore, in looking for synonyms, do it by completing this sentence: *I am a "lukewarm" Christian when I am* _____ .

   1.   6.
   2.   7.
   3.   8.
   4.   9.
   5.   10.

 2. Rev. 3:18 presents the *constrast* to lukewarmness, thus we have the opposite of it presented. What Christian-life qualities do you think is meant by:
   (1) "Gold refined by fire"? Would this mean "purity"? Or what?
   (2) "White garments"?
   (3) "Salve to anoint your eyes"?

*3. Rev. 3:20 is often misused to represent Christ calling the unsaved. It is really Christ calling to a church (thus, Christians) who have crowded Him out! He wants in the *fellowship* with them. List some things which are necessary for our fellowship with Christ.

   1.   6.
   2.   7.
   3.   8.
   4.   9.
   5.   10.

*4. If the above #3 is true, which item on the list do you need *most* to do to improve your fellowship with Christ?